D0906907

Advance Praise for *Purpose*

"Karen Hoyos is a true example of success: From coming to the US with nothing, to building a multimillion-dollar company, all through helping people to fulfill their purpose! The best part is that this book will show you *how*!"

—Bill Walsh, America's Business Expert

"Karen's transformational book will empower you to live your legacy and make powerful contributions to the world!"

—Liz Stern, Legacy Expert, Globetrotter of 95 Countries

"*Purpose* will elevate your consciousness and transform your personal and financial life forever."

—Rocio and Alfonso Martinez, Real Estate Investors

PURPOSE

THE ULTIMATE QUEST

KAREN HOYOS

A POST HILL PRESS BOOK
ISBN: 978-1-68261-807-3
ISBN (eBook): 978-1-68261-808-0

Purpose:
The Ultimate Quest

Cover art by Tricia Principe, principedesign.com
Cover photo by Julian Serna, JulianSernaStudio.com
Dress by Lucia Rodriguez, LuciaRodriguezNYC.com
Hair & Makeup by Paolo Di Valdi, instagram.com/PaoloDiValdi/

Post Hill Press
New York • Nashville
posthillpress.com

Published in the United States of America

CONTENTS

ACKNOWLEDGMENTS

This book is a manifestation that has become a reality with the love, help, and support of many people. I extend my sincere appreciation to all of them.

First, I want to thank God for His grace, wisdom, and the peace provided throughout this journey. My thirty-nine years of life have given me all I need to fulfill Your *purpose* in my life.

I would like to express my gratitude and eternal love for my hearts and soul, my twins, David and Estevan. You are my heartbeat and my joy, and we have had over fifteen years of adventures together. I am so proud of the intelligent, conscious young men that you have become and look forward to seeing how you both live your *purpose*. I am so blessed and so glad that you have been a part of my *purpose*. I love you with every part of me, and I am so happy to be your mom. Thank you for always sharing this crazy transformational life with me, even in challenging times. I love you with all my heart.

Thank you to my mother, Maritza, without whom my aspirations and dreams would not have reached fruition. You are my inspiration, my light, and my angel. I am so grateful for our relationship, our friendship, and our partnership. I love you, Mommy!

Thank you to my papa, Hernando. I have learned so many significant life lessons from you. I thank you for all you have done and for your legacy, love, and forgiveness in my life.

Thank you, Grandma Leto, you are the star of our family and you have taught me to share my light unapologetically.

Thank you to the man who raised me, who for me will forever be my dad, Raul Ospina.

Thank you to my sisters Jennifer and Natali, and my brothers Raul and Michael. You have been extraordinary teachers for me. I am so grateful to have you in my life. Ivonne, you are an amazing sister. When you were born, I was already fifteen! You gave me the gift of practicing how to be a mother. I am grateful for all your experiences and for my precious niece, Athena! She, along with Brisa and Maximus, are my little stars. Thank you *Tio* Rafael, Marlon, Estefania, Diana, and Titi.

Thank you my *peluche* family, the Martinez family: Rocio, Alfonso, Alfonso Jr., and my bright sun, my goddaughter Ariana. You are the manifestation of love and miracles, and you epitomize the definition of family. You are my angels and we are together, forever. *Los amo!*

I am highly appreciative of the support of those who believed and invested in the vision of this book: Rocio and Alfonso Martinez, Gary Salvit, Dawn Diaz, Gerald Surya, Juan Plaza, Marcela Cordoba, Leonardo Manrique, Luz Cuellar, Juan Restrepo, Mario Quiroz, Naidy Quiroz, Jacqueline Muller, Hanna Garduño, Paola Pineda, Pierangela Marinucci, Liz Stern, and Susana Koehler. Thanks to you, this powerful transformational tool for the world is possible.

ACKNOWLEDGMENTS

I am so appreciative of my Karen Hoyos International family who embody our slogan of *Leading Leaders*. We live with passion and manifest our *purpose* together; without you none of this would be possible. Thank you, Doctor Alba Corzo for being pure light. Paula Ronderos, thank you for being my true friend and for being with me since my first super team.

Special thanks to my soul sister, Ambassador April Sutton. Your wisdom and commitment to global transformation and humanitarian efforts are evolutionary and awe-inspiring. You continue to change the world through your global partnerships and I thank God for our unique and special life connection.

A special thank you to my Chief Operations Officer, Tiffany Edwards, for an unconditional commitment to this mission of *purpose*, diversity and inclusion, nonstop work, sleepless nights, and being a crazy leader like me! Your inspirational dedication, credibility, and the outstanding level of hard work ethic are an unexpected blessing in my life.

Thank you to my mentor Gary Salvit for helping me transform my spiritual relationship with prosperity.

A big thanks to the production team of this book's beautiful jacket cover. My hair and makeup on the front cover were styled by master celebrity artist Paolo D. Validi.

Thank you for all the laughs and special moments we share! You are forever in my heart. My dress is by the one and only Lucia Rodriguez—your work is pure Essence! Thank you to the extraordinary Julian Serna for the amazing photography. My back-cover hair and makeup are by the amazing Catalina Jimenez, with hair and makeup support by the one and only angel, Jenny Arreaza. My dear Marcela Ramirez, thank you for providing and being my ongoing Leader support.

Thank you, JD Films DP, for the great cinematography behind the scenes of the shoot of the Purpose cover. For impeccable production by top leader Juan Restrepo—thank you, love, for sharing your soul!

Thank you to my dear Dawn Diaz. I am grateful that you said *yes* to your calling and for walking so many paths with me, including the beginning of the manifestation of this book. I am appreciative for Milagros Day as the first tangible manifestation of Purpose, and healing through coaching.

Orlando Tobòn, I will be forever grateful for you being the first person to believe in me. You put me on a stage in front of five hundred life-sentenced inmates. To the first producer to put me on national TV, thank you, Jesùs Becerra, for seeing in me the end product. Thank you to my dear friend and small business coach Bill Walsh for giving me the opportunity to share the stage with names in the industry that were once my mentors, like my dear Les Brown and Brian Tracy.

Thank you so much to the incredible Ascendant Group for giving me the opportunity to shine my light through this book. Raoul Davis, thank you for believing in my God-given *purpose*. Leticia Gomez, as I teach in this book, you are a badass angel and awesome agent.

Thank you to my publisher, Post Hill Press, and its amazing team. Anthony Ziccardi, Debra Englander, and Madeline Sturgeon, thank you for your patience with the birth and through the challenges during the materialization of this book. Thank you to my distributor, Simon & Schuster, for allowing me the opportunity to reach, teach, and transform the lives of millions of readers!

I wish to extend a heartfelt thanks to all the graduates of my seminars for trusting your Essence and choosing a life of transformation and *purpose*. Because of you, I am here. You are the example of what is possible. Thank you so much to every person who believed in me and their *purpose*, opened a door, and gave me an opportunity to share my mission. I also want to thank those of you who didn't believe or tried to put me down, for because of you, I am stronger.

Thank you, my beautiful country Colombia, I am with you wherever I go. This book exists to inspire every person who has a vision bigger than themselves.

Now I thank *you*, the special being reading this book, for making a dream a sweet reality. I am appreciative of you being part of the transformation of this beautiful planet, for choosing to see with the eyes of your Essence, and for giving me a chance to dance with your soul!

Gracias de Corazòn,
Karen Hoyos

FOREWORD

BY AMBASSADOR APRIL SUTTON

This book is a roadmap to help you find your *purpose*. There are many people around the world who are wondering and asking themselves why they are here, and some others may feel they are not reaching their highest potential. They have their searchlights on and they are trying to find themselves.

After reading this book, perhaps you will not have to wonder anymore. This book is written to help people find themselves. For those people who are seeking to discover their *purpose*, this book and Karen are the answer! Karen specializes in personal evolution and boundary breakthroughs.

Purpose is a must-read book that provides effective steps to self-discovery. Karen is a top motivational speaker leading a powerful motivational movement across the globe. She leads a diverse, multicultural company filled with awe-inspiring leaders committed to helping others. This book is a tool that provides a blueprint of Hoyos' live teachings that continue to inspire, motivate, and transform the lives of masses of people seeking to reach their highest potential.

PURPOSE

Karen's reach is global, and her dynamic approach in empowering people garners extraordinary results. People who have diligently engaged in the process of finding themselves and their *purpose* discover they can reach higher levels of self-awareness. *Purpose* is for people who are open minded and willing to dig deeply into self-examination, positive introspection, and spiritual enlightenment.

This book is a positive reflection that mirrors her extraordinary life. Karen's teaching is intercontinental, interdenominational, multicultural, and can benefit anyone. Karen's life is filled with an unquestionable commitment to the highest professional ethics and integrity. This, along with her infectious charisma, ensures that those in need are reached and aligned with their newfound *purpose*. It is this ability that Karen uses in her commitment to help people discover why they are here.

Imagine ten thousand people sitting in a stadium waiting for one woman to hit center stage. The woman they are eagerly waiting for is from Colombia, South America, who has been empowering masses of people, bringing hope, inspiration, and confidence to people who are searching to find themselves.

This is the opportunity where many people can meet my dear friend, Karen Hoyos. She is a motivational speaker, philanthropist, and humanitarian who has become a major force in finding solutions and answers to life's frustrations. Karen, like millions of people across the globe, has experienced major challenges, yet she has found a way to push forward despite the most devastating of setbacks.

FOREWORD

As a single parent, raising two young boys and taking the leap from South America to North America has not been an easy feat. However, today Karen stands boldly and speaks fervently about her life and solutions that have transformed her, forever.

I first met Karen years ago at a social function in Beverly Hills and it didn't take long for me to recognize that I was in the presence of an extraordinary soul. Life's mysteries often surprise us when we stumble across an individual who is supposed to be in your life forever. These uncanny moments always take us by surprise. But through the many powerful people that I have met throughout my life, Karen Hoyos perfectly fits the description of what has been a consistent pattern in my life. Let me explain.

There are some people who are destined on this Earth to find themselves in front of people who sit in high places. People who are leaders, top celebrities, and influencers. There are also individuals who are destined to stand before not only these leaders and influencers, but also people from every walk of life and become a beacon of hope and a guiding light for all of them. Karen has been a shining light helping people to push through depression. Through my special relationship with Karen, I have witnessed the impact she has had on many diverse people who have been searching to find their life *purpose*.

I have personally listened to countless testimonials of individuals expressing their gratitude to Karen. They have benefited tremendously from her helping them through depression, transitions, and life's uncertainties. The seminars she conducts consistently bring positive results. Millions of people are flocking to attend Karen's live seminars and workshops. Her bestselling products are tools for those who may never be able to attend a seminar or see her in person. This book is one of those tools.

Karen gives an intimate account of how her personal difficulties and trials became triumphs. Through this book, you will find masterful methods to self-discovery. Join her in finding that your life *purpose* is a reachable goal. Explore the formula to your successful future in this compelling, must-read book.

To your *purpose*-driven life,
Ambassador April Sutton

INTRODUCTION

The moment I found my purpose, I found the gift of contribution. I discovered that humanity is shifted by the honor of love and service. I have been blessed to be a vehicle to many powerful causes and, within that, I have transformed my own life. Contribution is the only evidence I will ever need of my existence.

I dream that my humble impact will stay alive far beyond my time on this planet. I have discovered that it is every person's birthright to be happy. This happiness is found by living our purpose and giving a hand to those in need!

Every time we are feeling low, we must help each other. I invite you to find your calling within the generosity of your soul and manifest your legacy for this world. Do not wait; your time to give is now.—Karen Hoyos

The journey of billions of people on this planet begins with them wandering around aimlessly, slaves to their own Ego and their own confusion about why they're here. It summarized my existence also until only a few years ago. I was confused and lost in the darkness of my profound fear and suffering, until the moment when everything changed.

A MOMENT I'LL NEVER FORGET

He stood over me with a gun to my head. I thought, "I am about to die at the hands of the man I love." I started praying, "Please God, help me, I don't want to die!" During my desperation, I promised myself that if I survived, I would change my life forever.

I saw his hand was being miraculously moved away from me as if a spell had been broken. The look in his eyes went from glazed and deranged, to shock and disbelief when he realized what he almost did to me. Tears of relief were running down my face.

That was the most challenging experience of my life. It was also one of the most important. It started me on the journey of my transformation. I walked away wounded, knowing deep inside my heart that I would find the answers to get rid of my pain. I realized I could not endure this agony. For so long, my existence had been blind to the core of my being. I didn't know myself. What I did know, however, is that I was destined for a *purpose*, and I was determined to find it.

PURPOSE: THE ULTIMATE QUEST

As I look back at that lost woman from years ago, I would not have thought she would achieve success and recognition as a global transformational leader, celebrity coach, coach of coaches, speaker, and author. It is humbling to be blessed with experiences that I could not imagine in my wildest dreams. My commitment to serve has given me the privilege of sharing my message on powerful stages, including Harvard University, Carnegie Hall, and the United Nations. My company has become a source of transformation for millions of people worldwide through our seminars, television show appearances, published articles, and products.

My vision to reach the masses has led me to coach influential leaders and Hollywood stars. As their lives are transformed, so are the lives of those who seek to emulate them. As a result of my successful interaction with personal development and corporate and entertainment industries, I have been featured on covers of international magazines, and as a special guest on some of the most recognized red carpets, such as the Grammy Awards and the Oscars. However, I am very clear that the glamourous aspects of my life are only a small part of the grand, divine plan to fulfill my mission.

I will forever remember how God orchestrates everything for me to find my *purpose* and how He placed an angel in my life who took me to my first personal development seminar. When I saw the speaker on stage transforming the lives of thousands of people, including mine, I heard God's voice in my heart. "*That*," He said, "is what you are going to do for the rest of your life!" I found my ultimate calling: to empower people to find their *purpose*.

The moment I said *yes* to that calling was the moment that my *purpose* came alive, and in the process, its manifestation began. I realized that I had to transform my own life first and become congruent to guide others through the journey of transformation. I became a product of my own message.

"Be the change that you want to see in the world."—Gandhi

Over the next few years, I invested everything I had into learning the craft and industry of personal growth, business strategies, media relations, and anything that would help me bring my message of transformation to the masses. I acquired all this knowledge while immersing myself into deep spiritual teachings and connecting with God through my own Essence. Through this combination, my life became a reflection of the practical spirituality that I teach today.

This book, like my seminars, goes much deeper than motivation. It works at the core of people's Essence. It will present you with a key that goes beyond happiness. It is the key of peace, joy, freedom, and bliss. When you *Find* your *purpose*, it opens your eyes to a new, expanded gratitude. When you *Live* your *purpose*, abundance in all areas of life becomes possible, and obstacles are merely challenges that can be overcome. When you *Share* your *purpose*, the pure joy of contribution gives you an unparalleled sense of fulfillment.

PART I

FIND IT

This book will only land in the hands of those who are ready. You are reading this book about *purpose*...on *purpose*. Throughout history, humans have sought to answer the questions, "Who am I?" and "Why am I here?" There is no greater quest in life than finding one's calling and choosing to live it, and there is no greater satisfaction than sharing it with others and honoring it forever. Every person on this planet has a *purpose*. We all share a collective *purpose*, yet the manifestation of it in our lives is an individual process. Life reveals that each mission is divinely connected. You may fit into one of these categories:

- You don't know what your *purpose* is, and you are ready to find it.
- You already know what your *purpose* is, have no idea how to live it, and you are committed to start living it now.
- You are living your life's *purpose*, and you are ready to expand the impact of your mission on this planet.

PURPOSE

It is my honor to coach you through the process of finding the answers you seek about *purpose.* For this process to be effective, you and I must make an agreement:

1. Do not simply believe what I present to you in this book. Rather, I invite you to verify these principles yourself by fully putting them into practice.

2. I know you are intelligent, and you have a brilliant brain; however, the understanding of this book goes far beyond your mind. Therefore, my communication with you will be through your heart—not your head.

3. It is important to acknowledge that your mind may want to judge and doubt what your heart is discovering. I ask you to trust your instincts and allow your heart to recognize the truth that is already within you.

4. When the little voice in your head says, "I already know this, I don't need this, I'm not ready for this," or "I can't do this," you will say to it, *"Thank you for sharing."* If you are saying to yourself, "What little voice is she talking about? Maybe she's crazy, I should stop reading this book!" Well, that is exactly the little voice I'm talking about. That is your Ego!

5. I want you to have fun! Just because we are talking about something this deep doesn't mean you must be so serious, so locate a mirror near you right now and smile! Just relax and enjoy.

CHAPTER 1

The Ultimate Question

Years ago, a woman came to my life in critical condition. She was not looking for motivation or even happiness. All she wanted was to stop the deep, intense pain that had taken her to the point of not wanting to live. She had tried it all, and she was inconsolable.

Hundreds of therapy hours and countless seminars later, she remained in a constant search that only took her to the depths of depression. The more knowledge she accumulated, the more she hated herself and her life from the desperation of not being able to apply what she had learned. I knew her life was in a state of emergency. I also knew that her life was about to change forever.

From within her darkest hour, and following the last glimpse of light she could see, this woman gathered the strength to be able to hear the ultimate question: What is your *purpose*?

ESSENCE REMINDER

Spiritual and scientific sources have found that currently only 1 percent of the world's population is fully living their life's *purpose*. They have discovered a formula projecting that when this percentage increases to 3 percent, the entire planet will be shifted to a level of consciousness where peace will be possible.

YOUR LIFE'S *PURPOSE* IS TO EVOLVE AND TO CONTRIBUTE

Evolution

Evolution means change, transformation. This is reflected from the slightest movement of the Universe, to the trillion cells within your body, and each experience of humanity. Evolution has always existed; we cannot stop it. Our destiny is to evolve. You may now recognize that everything that has happened in your life has been part of a perfect plan. Therefore, everything that happens on this Earth is in perfect order. Throughout history, humans have evolved consciously and unconsciously.

Conscious evolution is a choice, choosing to learn, grow, and understand the reason for your existence. It is exactly what you are doing by reading this book. The first glimpse of conscious evolution is the surfacing of such existential questions like, "Who am I?" and "Why am I here?"

Unconscious evolution occurs when people live a life where their circumstances dictate their results. They feel they are at the mercy of situations and of other people's actions, living as victims of their own lives. Although they are still experiencing change, it is a painful way to evolve. This is the way most people live. They are blinded by a veil that wraps them in suffering.

My life's *purpose* is to awaken human consciousness, through *purpose*, so that more people chose to evolve consciously and transform the quality of our human existence into one of harmony, peace, and love.

Contribution

Contribution is to serve. We are all contributing, consciously or unconsciously, to the evolution of humanity.

Conscious contribution refers to our conscious choice. We contribute to ourselves, to others, and to causes that support the individual and collective transformation of our planet. We can see references of conscious contribution in our everyday lives. From the smallest measures of contribution, like a genuine smile, greeting a stranger, or helping someone in need, to historic acts that have had the deepest impact on our society as carried out by great leaders like Mother Theresa, Gandhi, and Doctor Martin Luther King, Jr.

Unconscious contribution refers to the impact of the actions that we take in our own lives that contribute to lowering the vibration of humankind. This is a "default" state, in which people believe that none of what individuals say or do has an impact on the rest of the world. The reality is that everything and everyone matters.

Each one of us is responsible for our surroundings. For many, this becomes a hard cookie to digest. "How can I be responsible for the suffering of humanity?" they ask. "How can my actions be contributing to wars of the world?" Well, if you are not at peace within yourself and with the people around you, you are generating violence on the planet. Period.

Only by taking responsibility for every result in our life, for everything and for everyone, can we truly have a choice to make a difference. To find the answer to the ultimate question of one's true *purpose*, we must remember that we each have our own powerful and unique God-given gift. This gift is the vehicle through which our *purpose* is manifested in all its glory throughout the Earth.

How do we really know what our gift is and what our calling is? Answering the following series of questions has made it possible for the thousands of graduates of our seminars to clarify their life's *purpose:*

A. If you had all the money in the world and all the time to enjoy it, what would you do with your time? (Your time, not your money!)

B. How would you use it to serve others?

C. If you didn't have to be concerned about paying bills, what would be the focus of your work?

D. What are you most passionate about?

For some people, the answer would be to become a singer, teacher, doctor, coach, or healer. Others may say a carpenter, pilot, or scientist. The important thing is to recognize that your calling has been given especially to you because you are the chosen one for it. You will never be fulfilled until you are living it fully!

> *"In modern spirituality, the definition of living your purpose is doing what you love the most, using it to serve others, while creating financial abundance for you and for them—both for profit and nonprofit."*—Karen Hoyos

LET'S *BE* THIS

Congruence is at the foundation of every principle you are receiving from this book. Only when you put fully into practice what you are learning here will you have access to the results that are in store for you. Follow these steps:

1. Close your eyes and slowly breathe deeply in and out through your nose three times.

2. Open your heart and welcome the answers that are ready to be discovered.

3. Feel the answers. *Do not think about them!* Approach these tasks from your Essence and not from your mind.

4. Answer the Ultimate Question, "What is your *purpose*?" Use these questions as your guide:

- If you had all the money in the world and all the time to enjoy it, what would you do with your time? (Your time, not your money!)
- How would you use it to serve others?
- If you didn't have to be concerned about paying bills, what would be the focus of your work?
- What are you most passionate about?

5. Write down your answers in powerful and concise statements that clearly describe your life's *purpose*.
6. Be grateful for your newfound clarity.
7. Share your *Purpose Statement* with ten or more people over the next twenty-four hours, *with passion*!

SUCCESS STORY

The woman who inspired the first story in this chapter, Dawn Diaz, is one of many great examples of the impact of Karen Hoyos International's coaching and training. She has experienced the two extremes that can mark the end or the beginning of a person's life, from wanting to die to a state of true happiness by living her *purpose*.

Through my coaching and seminars, Dawn courageously healed a lifetime of abuse and childhood trauma, manifested the vision of her calling, and transformed her life and the lives of many others. The impact of her *purpose* is palpable in the world today as an international speaker, author, life coach, and founder of the nonprofit organization Milagros Day Worldwide.

Dawn Diaz's Testimonial: *Karen always speaks to my greatness and holds me to the highest standards; she never accepted the limitations I place on myself. She constantly challenges me to break through the barriers of my comfort zone and put my* purpose *into immediate and massive action. If you are ready to make your dreams come true and are ready to feel the pure joy of gratitude and contribution, then Karen Hoyos is the coach for you!*

As you start walking your *purpose*-filled path, you will have access to a life that you really love. You will recognize that you already have everything you need, even though your mind will try to convince you otherwise, as you surrender to your calling. As you start embracing and choosing to live your *purpose*, the joy within your heart will be permanent—much more than mere motivation.

You will encounter true transformation. Everything will lead you to the most important part of all: *choice!* If only 1 percent of people on this planet are brave enough to shape their reality by living their life's *purpose*, the question you must ask yourself is: Am I ready to be part of the 1 percent today? If the answer is *yes*, I welcome you to a realm of infinite possibilities where you are the master of your destiny and God is the source of your manifestations.

CHAPTER 2

The Key to Happiness

Faith is the key to happiness, and every person on this planet is born with this key. The type of faith I am speaking of is not religious, although many religious people practice authentic faith. Rather, the faith that I am addressing expands beyond the mind and spiritual beliefs that support the knowledge that we are all here for a *purpose.*

Everyone has faith regardless of their origin of birth, religious tradition, or socioeconomic status. This faith does not stem from one's parents, or one's thoughts on what one deserves. This powerful key is a birthright and it is the Essence of what makes one human. This key is special for those who know how to use it. Most people are currently unaware of this key, which is why humanity is grouped based on their key knowledge.

ESSENCE REMINDER

Humanity is distributed into groups according to their relationship with their key:

- The Lost Ones
- The Seekers
- The Spectators
- The Braves
- The Defeated
- The Chosen Ones

THE LOST ONES

The Lost Ones are unaware they possess the key. They are not aware or present in their existence. You may find them in the streets, lost to drugs and alcohol. They have lost their ability to see beyond the density of their minds.

My sister Jen is a beautiful girl who was filled with energy and passion for life. We are two years apart in age and I was a part of almost every aspect of her life. Growing up, I saw her morph from a laughing, happy, engaging, beautiful butterfly into someone whom most people can barely recognize.

When Jen was little, a trusted family member cruelly attacked her innocence and sexually molested her. My family and I didn't know for a long time because she stayed silent and kept it from all of us. Jen also had another secret that she kept locked away: She is a lesbian.

It is no surprise to me that my sister is a lesbian. I fully love and support her. She is gay, and that is okay. I believe in equality and that God makes us all perfect just the way we are, regardless of whom we love, what we look like, and what we choose.

Jen is extremely smart, and like many smart people, her mind was filled with voices. These voices inside her head would scream at her that she was not enough, that she was bad, that she and her choices of whom to love were dirty. She didn't know that the voices were her.

She was fifteen years old when she began destroying her life with drugs and alcohol. She left home, running away from herself until she couldn't find her way back. She spent years in and out of trouble, in and out of jail, consuming substances in an attempt to quiet her mind. The more she tried, the more she was losing herself.

My family and I did everything we could to help her. We tried several mental health centers and gave her holistic cures and countless hours of therapy. Yet there was a time when Jen chose not to come back. She stayed in a place where she could no longer fully exist because the pain was too much to bear. All of this happened before I found my *purpose.* When I discovered my ability to heal myself and others, it was painful to know I could help many people, yet my sister was gone.

I know firsthand the pain and suffering of this group. I have seen it with my own eyes, traveling the world and working with survivors of domestic violence, abuse, and many other atrocities. It takes only a quick look at the news to find there are so many Lost Ones in the world. Still, there is hope.

My mother and I accepted the difficult present reality that my sister was not the same, yet we didn't give up on her. We never will. She was able to clean her body from addictions and start living a normal life with a dear doctor friend who now is part of our family.

Jen is very special. Her emotional behavior is like that of a twelve-year-old. She is now thirty-six. She smiles and talks to herself a lot. She sings, dances, and loves to walk. Maybe one day she will catch up with her age, or maybe not. Even if she doesn't, the quality of her life has changed, as has her contribution to the world.

I believe the Lost Ones may contribute the most to humanity. This is because they give us hope, courage, and inspiration. Many of them will become living miracles, proving to the unconscious collective *Ego* that the power of Essence is always more.

THE SEEKERS

Seekers know they have the key, and they also know this key opens the door of their *purpose,* so they are *seeking* that door. Many go from one religion to the other, from book to book, seeking the answers to their questions. Some feel depressed and down, as if there is something missing. They can be sometimes happy, but not fulfilled. They are looking for *it.* Maybe you are. I know I was.

It was a rainy night. I had an introductory seminar in New York. Despite the weather, a crowd of two hundred people were there. They were ready, they were seeking. I delivered a training seminar from my heart.

It moved people to tears and into action. People usually approach me at the end of these training seminars to thank me and share their breakthroughs. This time, however, I saw something powerful in the eyes of one participant.

Alfonso Martinez was reluctant to attend. He told his wife Rocio not to go to the seminar and focus on making money instead, for they were in the worst financial situation of their lives. His heart was searching for answers.

Alfonso and Rocio were self-made millionaire realtors who lost everything when the real estate market crashed. They were looking for a strategy to come back, yet their soul key holder was looking for their *purpose* door.

Alfonso ran to me and looked directly into my eyes. "I found *you*," he said. "I was looking for this. You will be my coach for the rest of my life!"

Wow, quite a declaration. "So be it," I replied.

One year later, they recovered everything they lost and gained much more. Alfonso and Rocio became successful real estate investors, coaches, and speakers. They graduated from all my training seminars and conference and joined our team of leaders. They found their calling to make a difference on the world. They healed their past and created a beautiful present for themselves and their amazing children, Alfonso, Jr., fifteen, and Ariana, who was in Rocio's belly at the time.

I am proudly Ariana's godmother, and as the years went by we became a family. They are my best friends, with whom I have shared more than a decade of love, fun, and a lot of coaching.

Seekers are pointers to the most important questions. They are insatiable because they understand there's more to life than what they see with their eyes. They are rebels and challenge what most people will accept. They are hungry and ready to go...or will they really go? Seekers have a powerful mind and with it a strong Ego that convinces them that they are not ready, that they may have to search a little more. Many of them doubt themselves, for their Ego says, "You are not there yet." If you want to want to fully live your *purpose*, you can't remain a seeker. You must find the door, be brave, and enter. For those who are choosing to continue, there is more.

THE SPECTATORS

Spectators are a sophisticated group because they *know*. They have found their *purpose* and located the door. Spectators are usually highly educated, both conventionally and informally. They may be seminar participants, read personal development books, and have eloquent conversations about what is possible through legacy and transformation. They have the tools to change the world, know the steps necessary to take, and they even have a perfect plan for it.

Spectators are usually found in groups, leadership projects. They have access to a beautiful window next to the *purpose* door. These people can clearly see what is on the other side: the happiness, abundance, freedom, and love. They see their *purpose* so well through the big and clear window that they have forgotten to open the door.

They are comfortable with the lives they lead; good lives, some with good jobs and living not exactly how they want, of course, yet have exactly what their Egos need to keep them trapped where they are. This is a dangerous place to be, many of them stay years and years in this comfort zone.

"Carlos" (to protect his privacy), is very charismatic and has the power to influence people around him. Carlos is dynamic, and his positivity and passion conquered my heart. We began dating.

He was a coach and speaker like me. We shared the same door, yet we used our keys differently. While he was passionate about sharing the message of his *purpose,* at the same time he was the CEO of a major company that afforded him a secure salary and a comfortable life. One day I asked him, "If you had all the money in the world and all the time to enjoy it would you still be the CEO of this company?"

"No," he replied emphatically. "I would only dedicate my life to doing what I love."

This smart and capable man was willing to trade his precious time for money and perceived financial security.

"Why not follow your heart and your *purpose*?" I asked him. I wanted to know if he was willing to let go of the illusion of security and follow his heart.

"I will only do it for you," he responded. "I want to make you happy, but making that type of change would be for you, not me."

It was not appropriate for me to accept his offer to change his professional life to please me. His transformation must come from his calling to his *purpose,* not for what he thought I wanted or needed. I believe in the freedom to choose and create our own destiny for ourselves. One needs to decide to make *purpose* driven choices based on a shift in consciousness, not in the desire to please a loved one. I decided our values were too different and that we could be great friends, not life partners. What is it that makes someone go for what one wants, while others who can lead a *purpose*-driven life, will not make the same choice?

"Leap and grow your wings on the way down," my dear friend Les Brown said. How can you really do this? After reflecting on this and having a conversation with a good friend, I realized it is a matter of faith. Blind faith that makes the Ego numb and doesn't know how to give up. This is the key. The key to happiness is the key of faith.

THE BRAVES

This group has found their *purpose* and they have chosen to use the key and open the door to follow their dreams. They have gone beyond their own fears, and in many cases faced the criticism of others and embarked on an unknown path.

I was participating in one of the hundreds of trainings and seminars that I attended in my own quest to fulfill my calling. It was the last day of a retreat when I stopped to get a cup of water. I found myself dancing to celebrate the culmination of a transformational weekend! I love dancing, by the way.

I found myself near a beautiful, petite woman who was asking someone to translate from English into Spanish. I immediately interceded to help her. She was pleasantly surprised because she thought I was Middle Eastern. She didn't know that I also was Latina and a native Spanish speaker. Stephanie Fiallo and I became instant friends.

PURPOSE

Stephanie is originally from Ecuador, a neighbor to my native country, Colombia. We share the same passion for life, growth, and contribution. We decided to meet in New York after the training and spent time sitting in a cafe laughing and enjoying delicious tea. Inevitably, our conversation touched upon my favorite subject: *purpose*.

At that time, Stephanie had spent fifteen years in a stable job and salary and had a good life. She was working as Human Resources Director for a well-known college in New York. Yet she had not found her *purpose*, so the passion for her job and the fire of her mission were missing.

I asked her my favorite question. "Stephanie, if you had all the money in the world and all the time to enjoy it what you would do with your time to help others?" She immediately replied, "I would help couples to have extraordinary relationships. I would help individuals find their soulmates and help humanity heal their personal relationships."

She recognized she was already a relationship coach without even knowing it. She had helped hundreds of people for over a decade, saving marriages from divorce, and introducing couples that eventually married. She had studied thousands of hours about the art of love, sex, and relationships. She finally had the clarity of her *what* but of course she didn't know the *how*.

Stephanie is one of *the braves* who made the leap. She used her key to open the door of her *purpose*. She often jokes that I turned her entire life upside down and destroyed her old life (in a good way, of course) to build it back with her dream life. She quit her job, overcame many challenges, became a certified coach with me, and continued her training. She launched her relationship coaching company and has been so successful in the past years that she received international notoriety. *Oprah Magazine* chose her from over three thousand women as one of the eighty most influential leaders in the USA. She is a living example of *the braves*. Stephanie grew out of her comfort zone and was willing to let go of the good to welcome the extraordinary. Today she is living the life of her dreams.

This opportunity is not only for some people, it's for everyone who chooses to use their key and open the door to their *purpose*. It takes courage to go beyond the fears of the mind. "What if…?" is the Ego's favorite limiting question. Don't let your Ego stop you from going after what is in your heart. On the other side of the door you can find the treasures that God/the Universe has for you.

THE DEFEATED

How can it be that right next to *the braves* you find *the defeated*? The defeated were once braves who lost their way. It's not enough to open the door, it's not enough to follow your dreams. You must be and do whatever it takes to stay focused and face the inevitable fight between Ego and Essence. As soon as you start living your mission and your faith gets stronger, your Ego will too. This is the time in life where most people think they "got it" only to be surprised by a powerful Ego that will do everything to sabotage their way forward.

It is so important to understand who your Ego is and how it operates so it won't take you by surprise. In my seminars and coaching I always train people to have a close relationship with their Ego. Many religions and practices seek to destroy the Ego, but we can never fully do that. The Ego is an illusion of our mind; it won't be destroyed. Still, you can transform the influence that it has in your life. Enlightened people have an Ego as well, the only difference is that they don't identify themselves with it anymore.

In his all-time classic book, *Think and Grow Rich*, author Napoleon Hill tells the story of R.U. Darby. This story represents well the impact of The Defeated and what is on the other side for them if they have faith:

> *Darby's uncle had gold fever, so he staked his claim and started digging. After a lot of hard work, the uncle found a vein of ore, so he covered up his find and returned home to raise the money for the machinery that he would need to bring the ore to the surface.*
>
> *They raised the money and Darby travelled with his uncle back to the site to make their fortune.*
>
> *Things started well and before long, they had enough to clear their debts. They were excited, everything from here on would be profit and things were looking good.*
>
> *Then the supply of gold stopped. The vein of ore had disappeared.*
>
> *They kept on digging, but found nothing.*

After a while, they quit in frustration and sold their machinery to a junk man for a few hundred dollars.

After they went home in disappointment, the astute junk man called in a mining engineer who checked the mine and calculated that there was a vein of gold just three feet from where Darby and his uncle had stopped digging.

The junk man went on to make millions from the mine.

Darby returned home, paid back everyone who had lent him money and was determined to learn from his mistake in giving up too soon.

He went on to become a phenomenally successful insurance salesman, more than recouping what he would have made from the gold mine.

He learned the lesson that you need to persevere through difficulties and stay focused if you are to become successful.

Whenever you feel like giving up on your dream, remember that you may be just three feet from gold!

THE CHOSEN ONES

This is my favorite group. These world leaders are the ones shaping the course of humanity. They come in all forms, shapes, colors, and backgrounds.

These amazing souls have faced everything to fulfill their destiny, sometimes even death. They used their key to open the door, faced their dark side, cleaned up their space, and became congruent with their values and mission to finally discover the truth.

The truth is that the key does not belong to us. That key belongs to our Creator. Once we cross the bridge of doubts and uncertainty and we go beyond our fears of Ego we remember we must surrender and give back the key to the one who made it.

The chosen ones choose themselves and let go completely, leaving everything in the hands of God and the Universe while staying on *purpose* and taking intentional action. In this group you find Jesus, Buddha, Gandhi, Nelson Mandela, Martin Luther King, Mother Teresa, and thousands of unknown individuals who fulfilled their calling.

Once you give back the key to the Creator, the door of *purpose* disappears. There is no more going back, there isn't a plan B or C. The only option is to live your *purpose* despite the circumstances. People have asked me, "What would happen if you lost it all? Would you still be a coach?" I always answer that this has already happened to me.

After four years of living my *purpose* and helping people through seminars and coaching, I was completely broke. Graduates of my seminars were doubling and tripling their income, and I was watching my own income decrease.

I didn't understand how this could happen if I was doing everything "right." My financial situation was so "wrong." I soon learned that in life there aren't right or wrong results.

I often cried while praying to God, asking what I should do to resolve this financial situation. Like most people, I didn't know the *how,* didn't understand *why.* The situation became extreme and dire to the point that I couldn't pay my rent.

Imagine this: I was kicked out of my apartment with my twin boys, my sister, and my mother, and we didn't have anywhere to live. I had no idea what I was supposed to do. My Ego got loud. It told me all kinds of things to convince me to give up: *Find a job, your family will starve, you are a loser, how dare you to think you are good enough? You had beginner's luck,* you will never make it!

My body was shaking with the fear of my mind, but my heart was beaming with light! I used my circumstances to surrender completely. I let go of all control. I did not know what was going to happen.

I trusted God even when *everything* appeared to be collapsing in front of my eyes. As the book *The Alchemist* says, "When you follow your dreams the entire Universe conspires in your favor." Two angels in my life appeared.

I previously shared with you the story of Alfonso and Rocio Martinez as part of The Seekers group, about their financial transformation, and how they went from being broke to becoming millionaires in only one year of training.

This couple became my heroes and the manifestation of my own faith in one of the most difficult financial times of my life's *purpose.* I didn't have the money to pay the rent for my family. When they discovered that we were about to be homeless, they opened the doors of their home to us. They graciously said that I didn't have to pay anything to live with them. They told me, "keep helping people the way that you helped us."

My twin boys, my mother, my sister, myself, and our dog lived with them for nine months. Their presence was a manifestation of the fire of my soul, as my faith was untouchable like my results. This was truly a miracle and I knew that my destiny was to transform this planet through my message. I put God first and I had no other choice but to become my *purpose*. No turning back, no other options for me.

I met Gary, the man who became my mentor, as I connected deeper into my own relationship with God while still living with the Martinez family. A successful entrepreneur and self-made millionaire, he is one of the most spiritual people I have ever met. He taught me how to transform my spiritual relationship with money and to heal my connection with it. I realized that I was separating God from my business.

Many people are taught that money and the heart don't go together when the opposite is true. As I found the roots of my limiting beliefs, I opened the universal bank and made my first million dollars in less than three months.

In the past fifteen years, my business has grown into a multimillion-dollar business with over forty thousand graduates of my seminars. I now teach other coaches, entrepreneurs, and leaders how to be part of The Ones, how to heal their past and finally fulfill their destiny.

Only 1 percent of the population of this planet is living their life's *purpose*. Only 1 percent have done so much! And there is a formula that indicates when the 1 percent increases to 3 percent, the entire world will be shifted. I believe in that formula with all my heart. I know that for every life that is transformed, thousands will be touched as well.

My question to you is: Are you ready to find the ultimate quest and choose your *purpose*?

If *yes*, please take the following actions:

Homeplay:

Write Down:

1. Clarity is power: What group are you in right now in your life and why?
2. What are some of the limiting beliefs that may be holding you back from moving forward?
3. When (specific time) would you like to become part of the Chosen Ones?
4. If you are already part of the Chosen Ones, what can you do with your *purpose* to help others get there?

Now that you know where you are and what is so, what is next? Let's heal the past, transform your relationship with your Ego, and find your way to surrendering.

CHAPTER 3

Making Friends with Your Ego

INTRODUCING CARMEN: YOUR EGO HAS A NAME

The biggest obstacle preventing people from living their *pur-pose* is their relationship with their Ego. Many people try to use strategies to address the Ego like fighting, ignoring, or trying to control it. Those strategies do not work, and only make the Ego stronger. The most effective approach I have found to dealing with the Ego is to develop an intimate relationship with it. When we fully embrace and get to know it well it will no longer be able to run and control our lives.

I named my Ego Carmen, so I could identify when she was trying to control my life. The Ego can be invisible, and like a mask, we can put it on when needed if we understand it and how to control it. Most people do not know that this mask, their Ego, exists. Their Ego is operating behind the scenes and has a big personality! My life was a mess until I became aware of the existence of Carmen.

Now that I know Carmen exists, I can recognize when she is trying to run the show. Carmen is controlling, dramatic, and loves attention. It is all about her, everyone is wrong, and she is always right. For many years, I suffered because she was in charge. During my journey towards my *purpose*, I discovered that the Ego was created to serve us, and that every time that we acknowledge its presence, we are reminded of who we really are; pure Essence.

Yes, Carmen still exists, however, I now utilize her abilities in a positive way that contributes to my life's *purpose*. For example, when I am on the red carpet, in front of cameras, doing my hair and makeup, Carmen loves it and I honor that. Carmen opens the door, she gets people's attention, and once in the spotlight my Essence walks in. This gives me the opportunity to transform the lives of all the people she attracts. As you will discover, our Ego is really designed to be our partner.

When you embrace your Ego, you can use it positively to carry out the mission of your *purpose* with powerful results. Having a healthy relationship with your Ego allows you to lighten up and even have fun with its antics. This gives you access to compassion and generosity towards yourself and others, and to manifesting the fulfilling life that you deserve.

In the books *A New Earth* and *The Power of Now,* my dear friend Eckhart Tolle illustrates the impact of the Ego in our lives. Tolle says, "The most common Ego identifications have to do with possessions, the work you do, social status and recognition, knowledge and education, physical appearance, special abilities, relationships, personal and family history, belief systems, and often nationalistic, racial, religious, and other collective identifications. None of these is you."

All enlightened people have an Ego, they just do not identify only with it. To free yourself from the manipulation of your own Ego, you must first embrace it. As you accept that there is light and darkness in our minds, you learn to love yourself completely. You cannot find self-love while rejecting the parts of yourself that you do not like. Once you stop judging yourself, and making yourself wrong, you will find the strength in your heart to evolve, grow, and transform your life. You are perfect, and you are not broken, yet your Ego will do its best to tell you that is not true.

Do not miss living in the present because you are too busy listening to your Ego's voice. Realize that the voice you are hearing is your false self, the illusion of the mind that separates you from everything—including your own heart. Most people spend their entire existence living in their heads. Now that you are aware of your Ego, you do not have to live like this anymore!

My Ego started trying to convince me not to embark on my quest to fulfill my *purpose.* Carmen can be quiet and may come out when I least expect her. I try to ensure that I do not become fooled by Carmen. I have managed to quiet my mind for long periods of time and have been successful in helping my Ego to change forms. I know it will not go away. Once you start learning, developing, and using the coaching techniques on this book, your Ego will transform and become spiritual, so it will be patiently waiting until you think you have all aspects of your life under control to attack and take you by surprise.

ESSENCE REMINDER

Your Ego doesn't care if it hurts you or others. Your Ego may hurt the people that you love the most with the most passion because they represent love. True love is what disempowers your Ego.

Now what you do?

Against your Ego: *Nothing*, let me repeat this: *Nothing*.

To master your Ego: *Everything*. I repeat: *Everything*.

MASTERING THE FRIENDSHIP WITH YOUR EGO

Name Your Ego

It is vital that you name your Ego. Once your Ego is no longer a mystery, it loses much of its power. When you discover the name of your Ego, it is so much easier to recognize it when acting out. Call it out, thank it for appearing and reminding you of your greatness. Your Ego is *not* your enemy, it's not who you are at your core, it is simply your false self.

The Ego behaves like a little child. It is constantly seeking attention and looking for drama. It loves to be right and cause conflict. Despite all these challenges, your Ego can be your friend. When you embrace your Ego and know how to control it, you will begin to master your life. Choose to meet your Ego as a potential friend and find out his/her name, what your friend likes, and how your friend chooses to live.

To find out the name of your Ego take the following steps:

1. Close your eyes.

2. Breath in and out through your nose deeply.

3. Ask your Essence, God within you/your heart: God, what is the name of my Ego?

4. Listen and write down the first name that comes to you.

5. You can't think of a cool name or the name of a person you don't like! Otherwise, it would be the Ego naming itself. Let it come to you naturally. You will know when it comes.

6. When you hear the name, it won't make sense. You will laugh out loud because it is like finding someone when you are playing hide and seek.

7. Relax and enjoy the process.

8. Fun fact: You can have a female or masculine Ego regardless of your gender. Some women may have men's names or vice versa.

Know the personality of your Ego

It is important to know the personality of your Ego. Many people think that the Ego is thinking you are more than others or being arrogant. Even though this is true in many cases, the

Ego can also be shy, quiet, or indifferent. To know exactly the personality traits of your Ego answer the following questions:

1. Do you like to be in control or are you usually the victim of the situation?

2. Do you like to dominate conversations, or do you reserve your comments because you don't like confrontation?

3. Do you often get stressed about things or do you become apathetic and not care?

4. Do you love being the center of attention or you hate it?

5. Are you attached to winning? If you don't win, do you get upset, angry, or sad? Do you easily give up when things don't go your way, thinking is not meant to be for you?

On both sides of the questions listed above, the answer remains the same, these are traits of your Ego. Your Ego (Pablo, Sandra, Joe, Carlos, Jim, Jen, whatever you name your Ego) is trying to convince you that it runs your life and you. You must remember that your Ego is trying to control you, and this is not who you really are at your Essence.

Recognize the Rock

The Ego is not your enemy and it can be your friend. Many times in our lives, while being in survival mode or facing a difficult situation, we may have used our Ego to get a more "positive" result. I call this *The Rock*.

Examples of types of The Rock include:

- A spiritual Ego uses *The Rock* of unconditional love to let other people walk all over the person.
- A shy Ego uses *The Rock o*f supporting others to hide and not shine.
- A controlling Ego uses *The Rock* of influence to make people do to what it wants.
- A manipulative Ego uses *The Rock* of self-expression to make itself right and judge any person with different beliefs as being wrong.

The strategies of the Ego will wrongly coerce you to believe that there will always be winners and losers. Unless you are playing a game, remember that this is simply an Ego strategy to control you and make you think it's critical that you win, even if the person who loses is you.

This happens because the Ego loves to be right. It will do whatever it takes to keep you in one of two postures—either a victim or the aggressor.

Use Your Ego for Good

Every time your Ego says something negative to you, use it as a reminder of the truth. For example:

- The Ego says, "You are stupid."

  You reply, "Thank you for sharing and reminding me that I am brilliant."

- The Ego says, "You will never make it."

  You reply, "Thank you for sharing and reminding me that the time of God is perfect, and I am on my way!"

- The Ego says, "You are too fat, too ugly, too skinny, or too old."

  You reply, "Thank you for sharing and for reminding me that I am beautiful and perfect just the way I am today!"

- The Ego says, "You are a loser. Wealth, happiness, and true love are not for you."

  You reply, "Thank you for sharing and for reminding me that I am God in Essence, I already have it all!"

Homeplay:

Write down the phrases that your Ego says the most about you.

____

____

____

____

Now write down the Essence truth about each of these phrases here:

____

____

____

____

Thank you for reminding me that:

____

____

____

____

Ego/Essence Pointers

- Depending on the personality of your Ego, when receiving challenging news, it may react in ways that temporarily paralyze you. It can be angry, suffering, blaming others, or it becomes a victim. Your Essence will help you to act despite fear, look for a solution, take responsibility for your results, and find gratitude for the lesson learned within the challenge.

- Depending on your Ego's personality, when communicating with other people it may try to demand that you are right and dominate the conversation—not truly listening to others and simply waiting to reply. Your Ego will cause you to interrupt or shut down other people. It pretends that you understand, causes you to feel less than worthy, and tries to make you give up hope. It will try to make you disconnect. Your Essence will intently listen with respect and intention of understanding, not reacting. It will take a respectful stand for what it communicates, and will do so with power, clarity, and without excuses or judgment.

- When following your dreams and *purpose,* your Ego thinks it needs to sacrifice some things for others. It thinks it's impossible to have it all. Stressing out is one of your Ego's favored states, it believes that worrying is a symbol of caring. Your Ego has expectations, wants to control everything. It needs to know the exact plan, hates uncertainty, and doubts everything all day long. Your Essence is comfortable living with the uncertainty of not knowing exactly the *how* of things. It trusts the process and knows that everything is part of the plan to learn, grow, and move forward. It takes conscious action without being attached to the results. It learns from what does not work without making it wrong. Your Essence, who you really are, has blind faith and recognizes the power of *purpose.* Like the famous quotes from Paulo Coelho in his book, *The Alchemist*:

"And, when you want something, all the Universe conspires in helping you to achieve it."

"It's the possibility of having a dream come true that makes life interesting."

"One is loved because one is loved. No reason is needed for loving."

The *wanting* that Paulo talks about is going beyond your Ego's desires. This *wanting* is a recognition of your soul manifestations. Your Essence knows that you don't have to "go after" your dreams. You simply allow them to materialize; everything that is in your heart is already yours. The Essence doesn't fear competition, for what is yours no one can take away from you.

The Eye Above: Ego vs Essence

I always practice the following: I picture that I have a big eye on top of me. This is the eye of an observer: the eye of my own Essence. This means I am observing who I am being in every moment. Am I being my Ego or my Essence? When making important decisions, stop thinking, breathe, observe yourself. Ask yourself, "Who am I being, Ego or Essence?" Declare what your Essence is going to do. Align yourself with what God wants you to do, listen, and then act.

Your Ego is your false self, it's who we think we are and it's the little voice in our head. It is the filter you use to see and experience the world. If you get to know your Ego more, you can learn to understand when your Ego is in control. To move into the direction of your *purpose* quest, you need to approach it from your Essence.

You cannot be driven by both Ego and Essence at the same time because they are two sides of the same coin. Your Essence and the Ego do not control with their power at the same time. When your Ego is in control, your Essence cannot fully be the driver of your actions. Conversely, when your Essence is guiding you, your Ego has no power.

True transformation comes from Essence. It is effective because it comes from integrity, it is prosperous, and has excellent results in life and business. There is no manipulation, there is no pushing, no conniving, only opportunities. Unless you know your Ego is present, we won't be able to live from Essence. We are all the same, we are one, 100 percent connected, fully present, here and now.

ESSENCE REMINDER

How do you understand when you are in Ego vs. Essence?

- Remember the difference: Ego is the false self, the person we think we are all the time.
- Essence is you 100 percent present (God, energy, love, light, etc.) It is your true self.
- Study closely your Ego characteristics, learn its personalities.
- Call the Ego by its name, acknowledge it when is active.
- Honor both sides. Own your Essence and embrace your Ego.

Feeding the Ego vs. Essence

Every day, our actions are feeding both our Essence and Ego. Ego and Essence are fed by what you see, read, watch, listen to, conversations you are having, thoughts you are entertaining, what you eat or drink, how you interact with people, what you do for a living, how you relax, play, and how you take care of your body.

The Ego loves to watch negative news, violence without a message or *purpose*, listen to dramatic songs, or novellas, especially if you're Latino like me. It loves to gossip, grimace, and not look people in the eyes. It feels guilty when relaxing and is stressed when working. The Ego will complain about pretty much everything. It doesn't care about health and will consume garbage or is simply not aware of what is being eaten. The Ego hates to move, work out, or dance. The Ego is always looking for food everywhere it goes.

Your Essence is pure and is constantly seeking a positive resolution and a way to contribute; it will not be inundated by what is going on in the world. It loves to laugh, joke, and not take life too seriously. Your Essence takes pleasure in making love, having orgasms, relaxing, and focusing when it's time to work. Essence does not complain, and if something is not working, it takes full ownership and takes the actions necessary to fix it.

Essence has the discernment to know when it is important to not take any action. Your Essence is patient, it does not gossip, and it clarifies directly with the person if something negative is in the space. Your Essence loves to clean up and Essence leads us to take care of our body.

An example of how my Essence helped me to transform and helped those around me is my choice to become vegan. Approximately fifteen years ago, I was seeking the most energy, the best health, and to help the planet and our animals. This led me to my choice to veganism. Essence has led me to make a healthy, ethical choice for my life that will impact those around me. My entire family also now is vegan.

Essence loves to dance, exercise, and invites us to move and live with passion. Essence connects us to our inner child. It reminds us to play and to let go. Your Essence honors everyone around you by greeting them with a smile, asking our waitperson for his/her name, showing gratitude by thanking people, requesting things nicely by saying *please*, opening doors, and helping people. These actions are not actions of expectation, they are the joy of service.

One Last Thing

As you recognize who you really are and unmask your own Ego, you also find compassion for others. You now understand that when you choose to do bad things, you are not bad, you were just unconscious and not aware of your own Ego. This doesn't justify your bad choices, but you now have an understanding and access to move beyond judgment of your choices. The next time someone says something mean to you or acts in a way that is not in alignment with you, do not take it personally. You know that it is not about you, it is about their Ego. Reflect on what part of your Ego is projecting the situation. Most likely it is not in the same area. I assure you that you will find an action you took from your Ego that is being mirrored by the person in his or her Ego.

As you take responsibility and start cleaning up your space, the people you will attract into your life will reflect your own Essence. The more you let your light shine, the more the reflection of love will illuminate your existence. Look around you. If what you see is not what you want in your heart, it is time to shift your energy and focus on your Essence.

PART II

LIVE IT

Purpose is happening in the present. To live one's *purpose*, one must heal from past issues. As we understand our past, we find the gift that it brings for us. Even the most painful and difficult moments are part of this gift.

Most people are lost in the pain of their past, carrying with them bags of negative experiences they have lived. Some may say, "I forgive but not forget." If you are still thinking about something that happened to you and feeling angry, upset, or disappointed in any way, then you haven't forgiven. You are pretending to be okay and avoiding the responsibility of truly healing.

Living your *purpose* is to be free to share your legacy. It's choosing to embody happiness, trusting the universal process, and being willing to see the perfection within the imperfect results of the mind's plans of our life. Suffering comes from our relationship with the past.

CHAPTER 4

Unwrapping the Gift of the Past

When I was four, I was playing in my room when I heard my mom screaming. I ran to the living room and saw my dad. The man who cared for me, whom I adored and trusted, was choking my beloved mother. His hands were around my mother's neck and his knee was on her chest. My whole world fell apart in that instant. I was scared and confused. What I unknowingly did next shifted my destiny. I grabbed a shoe and ran over to hit my father on his back. I was screaming at him to let go of my mother. When he saw me, he released his grip on her. I didn't know that this painful moment would became the source of the root of my relationship with men.

When I found my *purpose,* I realized that for me to transform other people's lives, I had to start with my own. I couldn't talk about being free and happy if I was still trapped in the experiences of my past. Yes, I could act like many coaches and speakers who are not congruent with what they teach, but I wasn't willing to do so. For me, congruence became my number one value.

I completed hundreds of seminars, including Landmark Education, Tony Robbins, Biodecoding®, meditation retreats, and many more. Through this process, I discovered that all the adversity my four-year-old self experienced was still running my life. I grew up wanting to live a different experience than my mother and not repeat my family's cycle of abuse. I saw this because my grandma also experienced domestic violence, and like both my mother and grandma, I ended up in an abusive situation. I am referring to the painful moment that I had a gun pointed at my head by the man I loved.

When healing my past, I discovered that when I saw my dad hitting my mother, I stopped trusting men. When I took my shoe into my hands and began hitting my father with it, I decided I was going to make men pay. This reflected in my life. I attracted abusive men, and I would cheat on them for revenge. I lived through this ongoing vicious circle until my *purpose* moved me to change my life.

BREAKING FREE OF SUFFERING

Healing your past doesn't mean you are justifying what happened to you. It does not make what happened right, or even wrong. Healing your past brings the perspective that nothing in life has a meaning, only the meaning our mind gives it. If you really want to make a change to transform your life and the lives of those around you, you must stop being a victim of your past.

The reasons you keep repeating the same results, attracting the same people, and continuing to suffer is because you are still thinking, "Why did this happen to me?" or, "This shouldn't be happening to me." You may think, "My past is wrong" or, "My life is wrong." Lastly, you may think, "The world's wrong."

ESSENCE REMINDER

You cannot change what you are judging as wrong. Only taking responsibility for your results and finding the root source of your results will allow you to heal your past and create something new.

You may be thinking this all sounds good but wondering *how* to do it. "How do I stop the pain of what I lived when I was young? How do I get rid of the anger that I have within me when I think about the man who raped me, the person who stole from us, or the women with whom my father cheated on my mom? *How*?" a person who was participating in my seminar asked me with tears in her eyes.

My answer: "When we stop asking *why* and instead ask *what for?* What is the *purpose* of this experience in my life?" When we ask these questions, we transfer from mind to Essence. While you may not find out the *why* of your experience, I can guarantee that you can find a *purpose* in everything that happened in your life if you are willing and open to discovering it.

After I found my calling, I understood the *purpose* of the painful experience of my past. I found many *purpose*s that I will share with you:

- First, I understood that for me to really connect with people and help them get rid of their own pain, they had to relate to me. They must believe that I understood what they are going through because I knew pain. I lived it.

- Many times, when people don't know anything about me, they jump to judge me and think that my life is perfect and filled with happiness and money. They do not know my story until I share it. Once that happens, a wall of resistance collapses and a true connection is presented and created.

- Because of my painful past, I now help many people. These people are moved and inspired by what's possible beyond abuse and survival. Your story, your pain, has value. If you are reading this book, it is because you have already faced challenges, experienced sadness or suffering. You are here because you didn't let that break you even if you are feeling broken right now. If you can look back and recognize what you did to overcome your situation and still be here, you can recognize a lesson that you can share with someone who may be in a similar situation.

- You don't need to be an expert to touch people's lives, your own life is all you need to inspire others if you are willing to see the gift within your past pain.

- Secondly, I understood that with the transformation of my relationship with my past, I could end the cycle of abuse in my family. Both my grandma and mother lived through domestic violence, and I did as well. When I took responsibility for this type of legacy, I addressed why I was unhappy, "incomplete," and resenting my past. I began to understand why I was replicating these issues in my own experience. I discovered that when you resist an issue, it will always persist until you heal it. I manifest this, so my Ego can keep the right of being a victim.

- This happens unconsciously, of course. No one wants to suffer. However, our Ego does. The Ego wants suffering, to be a victim, to control, it wants to be right. It doesn't matter if this will sacrifice your happiness because the Ego loves sacrifices. I know you may be thinking this makes no sense. You may ask how you can take responsibility for the abuse you experienced when there is someone else to blame.

- Blaming is the favorite game of the Ego—either self-blame or blaming others. Responsibility is when you say "I am no longer controlled by my past. I no longer allow what happened to me to define me. I don't condone this action, yet I know I manifest this with the lives of my own Ego and the collective Ego of my family."

- Although it is never okay to abuse a human being, and it was not okay that my father tried to choke my mother, I now understand that he was also driven by his own destructive Ego. When I stopped resenting my father, I

> found true forgiveness and I cut the chain of abuse in my life and those of future generations.

I found this healing when I was twenty-five. I invited my parents to meet me to have a conversation for the first time about our past. Here in front of me were two of the most important people in my life with so much pain in their hearts. My mother was desperate to leave her toxic relationship. She ran away with my sister and me when I was six. My father didn't know where we were and didn't hear from us until I was a teenager. He regretted his actions, and he wanted another opportunity to be a father. He didn't want to lose us, but he did.

He moved to the United States filled with grief because he lost the loves of his life, his daughters. He resented my mother for many years. Even when they met years later, my mom and dad were still carrying their reasons to hate each other…until the day I brought them together in my living room.

I started by asking both of my parents for forgiveness. They were confused because they felt there wasn't a reason for *them* to forgive *me*. Based on my new understanding of my *purpose*, I was aware of my responsibility and the role I played. I carried anger towards both of my parents, especially for my dad.

I resented my mom for turning me against my dad. Even though I understood her fear, I kept deep dark feelings in my heart. I hurt myself in relationships because I believed that I was broken based on the childhood I'd had. I unconsciously blamed them for my results. I took it upon myself to tell them that I was sorry for all that I felt and did.

They were both in tears. A big wall was destroyed right in front of my eyes. They both hugged me and cried nonstop for a while. My dad stepped up and asked for forgiveness from my mother. He addressed everything he did and all the pain he caused. He got down on his knees and wept at my mother's feet, and mine.

My father said he didn't understand why he had done what he did because he loves us. He acknowledged it was terribly wrong. My mom broke down and accepted his request. She forgave him. What happened after was even more magical. My mom asked my dad for forgiveness for all the hatred she had, and for running away with me and my sister and punishing him by taking away his right to be a father.

She asked me for forgiveness because she knew her actions had planted so many seeds of anger against my father. Then there was silence as the three of us stood there hugging, crying, healing, and breaking free from our pasts.

Today, I have completely recreated my relationship with my parents. At age thirty-nine I am writing this book, so I have benefited from having more than fifteen years of a transformed relationship with my parents. I am looking forward to more. We now share special memories together on holidays, birthdays, and Sundays, simply because we care about our family.

I love my mother and my father with all my soul. I can now see their contribution and the extraordinary wisdom they shared through their experiences. I continue learning from them, and because of our healing, many members of my family were able to do the same.

Transformation had a ripple effect. When my mom healed, my grandma decided to follow. For more than forty-five years, my grandmother carried feelings of guilt and anger. She suffered physical and psychological abuse at the hands of my grandfather. My grandparents married when my grandma was fourteen. Even while pregnant with my mother, he kicked her in the stomach. She suffered throughout the marriage.

My grandfather would assault her by hitting and punching her all over her body and her face. When my mother was about six, my grandmother mustered the courage to leave. She told my grandfather she couldn't take any more and that she was leaving him.

My grandfather told my grandma that if she left, he would kill himself. My grandma didn't believe him and left. Grandpa kept his promise, and after saying goodbye to my mom, he committed suicide by hanging himself.

Imagine the guilt and sorrow of my grandmother. My grandfather's side of the family blamed and hated her for his choice. My grandma never talked about his suicide and buried it within herself alongside my grandpa's memory.

Time marched forward and I became a speaker and a coach.

I invited my grandmother, mother, and aunt to attend one of my seminars. These three women used to be best friends until my grandfather died. That day at my seminar, they found closure, and within the space they created, the entire family surrendered to the power of love and healing. Now, almost fifty years of anger, hate, and darkness are where they belong—in the past, and a new beginning is present.

While healing in our families is possible, a member of our family must lead and take the first step. In my family, I was the one who took this on. You can do this too! It is not about convincing your family members, it is about inspiring them to see it. Your seed of love will impact your family and future generations forever. It is a matter of choice. Let's honor and embrace the quote of Rabbi Hillel about healing and transformation: "If I am not for myself, who is for me? And when I am for myself, what am I? And if not now, when?"

FINDING AND HEALING THE ROOT OF THE SUFFERING OF YOUR PAST

Homeplay:

This exercise can be used for any type of relationship in your past. No matter what you choose, make sure to include your parents. Your relationship with your parents is the foundation of every other relationship.

1. Choose the relationship you want to heal: mother, father, siblings, other extended family, close friends.

2. What is the result you want to change? Close your eyes and breathe deeply three times in and out with your hands facing up. Write the answer down.

3. Connect to your Essence, to your heart. Call out and ask, "God, (or your preferred deity) show me my root!"

4. Listen to the specific moment you were in that caused you to create the specific root. Write down and describe the experience by listing what you saw and how you felt.

5. Close your eyes again. Listen and recall what meaning and/or belief you created because of that experience. Examples: I can't trust anyone, women and men are the same, love means pain, and so on. Write down your personal meaning.

6. Acknowledge the impact. What has been the impact of having this belief in your life?

7. Take responsibility. Declare, "I am responsible!"

8. Are you willing to change it? Say, "I choose to transform my belief."

9. Go back to the moment and see it with the understanding of your Essence. What was the *purpose* of this experience? Write it down.

10. Which one do you choose?

11. What actions will you take to heal? Write down the names of the people involved and make sure you have a conversation to ask for forgiveness for whatever meaning and belief you carried. If the person is no longer alive, write them a letter.

12. Share your breakthrough with as many people you are able!

CHAPTER 5

Clean Up Your Poopoo

ESSENCE REMINDER

You can't put perfume on top of poopoo, for there is still poopoo underneath. You must clean the poopoo first and then create something new!

It is important that we are aware of the challenging circumstances we attract into our lives when we first say *yes* to our *purpose* and embark on a new journey and a higher level of consciousness. The collective Ego begins to throw wrenches into the mix. Thus, an avalanche of situations begins to occur, with the Ego trying to convince you that you are crazy for thinking this dream can be possible.

This is an illusion. Most people are stopped by these encounters and don't believe that all they must do is simply be themselves. The more you know and declare that with God on your side nothing can faze you, you become unbreakable. The collective Ego gets bored and tired of trying to throw you off your game. This is because you are *home.*

The attacks will become less frequent and dramatic, and sometimes they will become slicker and sneakier. Wherever I am, I am *home*, so I do not have to worry or protect myself from anything, just stay grounded.

To make sure we can stay grounded and focus in the manifestation of our *purpose*, we must keep the ground clean. Once we are fully responsible for everything that happens in our life, it will also become an emergency to start cleaning and completing this process with the people in our past and present. It is almost like an addiction for me (in a good way of course). I won't allow myself to coach, speak, train, or do anything that has to do with my *purpose* if my space is not clean, if I am upset, or if I am in my Ego about something that is unresolved. I declare: God, you think, speak, and act through me! When I do this, I let go of control and allow my higher self to take over. In life's challenges, there is always a gift.

As a transformational coach, this is one of the first distinctions we can have our clients awaken to, knowing that the circumstances of our lives and the lives of the people around us are references that give us clues to the root of patterns of suffering. These patterns teach us the lessons of growth and evolution. When those patterns can be identified, we can bypass the suffering mechanism and evolve consciously in a faster, more productive, and joyful way.

ESSENCE REMINDER

Cleaning up your space becomes like oxygen. It is the foundation of a life of *purpose*. The process of cleaning up is not only with others, it's also with yourself. One can't go without the other.

Some people would say, "That is just the way it goes" if you are still feeling upset about it or even having a small discomfort in your gut about something you haven't let go. It is within you. When people begin accumulating negative emotions that are not completely resolved, little by little these emotions will eventually evolve into sickness, and sometimes into lethal diseases.

I have a coaching client named Rosa. She was thirty when she first became involved with my training. She was a beautiful white woman with a distinct feature on her face—her nose was black. I didn't know the reason why her nose appeared the way it did until she explained to me that she had an advanced phase of cancer. The disease had caused damage to a lot of her skin tissue. Rosa was the youngest sister of one of the coaches on my official team.

When I found out about her situation, I knew I could help her. I offered her a cleaning coaching session and she agreed to participate. She was exceptional in the beginning. Once I connected to her, Essence to Essence, I was able to create a space of openness. She was ready. I never coach someone who is not ready because this becomes a manipulation of the Ego.

The difference between manipulation and influence is the intent behind our actions. I teach the coaches in my certification programs the importance of identifying the difference between those who are ready and those who are not as a process so everyone one involved is desirous of the change.

It was clear during the conversation in our coaching session that the person she was the most incomplete with (upset with, either consciously or subconsciously) was one of the people she loves the most, her sister Laura. I shared with Rosa that we could heal her cancer if we could identify the root process, she could heal herself. She agreed.

She shared her story with me, and many essential components needed to be present and essential in her healing/cleaning process.

Laura was always first in everything. She was the first child to be born and to receive their parents' love and attention. Laura was the first one to graduate, get married, and have a child. Rosa was always second.

In her heart, she was happy for her sister. Yet in her Ego, she felt less than worthy, and she wanted to excel at something. However, whatever she would attempt to do, Laura was ahead because Rosa intentionally would pick things Laura was already doing. Sometimes Rosa would be close to finishing before Laura, and Laura would always win by *a nose*!

"Wow," she said. "Laura would win *by a nose*!"

I remember this vividly. Rosa started crying hysterically, and Laura did too. She couldn't believe what she'd said. It was so difficult, yet it all suddenly made sense. As you can see from this significant example, this is the power of cleaning. You can now see clearly what was blurred by the fog of the Ego.

Rosa sincerely apologized to Laura for subconsciously being jealous of her. Laura apologized to Rosa for not being attentive to her sister's needs and for focusing so much on herself. They hugged for a long time and there was a sense of peace in the space.

What happened in the next four weeks was a true miracle. Rosa's nose cleared up, and the skin on her nose began to transition back to her natural complexion. Her doctor couldn't believe what he saw because there was no sign of cancer in her body. They just could not believe that without any medical treatment, she was healed. Well, I would say that there was treatment, just not a westernized medically accepted one.

Biodecoding® is the art of decoding the language of the cells to resolve effectively the emotional cause of illness, according to Christian Flèche. Sickness can be transformed into health when we find the emotional root that is causing it. I see this based on my results, the results of my life, and the lives of thousands of my graduates. The body is in constant communication with us. Your physical health is a great way to measure the status of not only your mental being, but your emotional well-being too. When we don't clean up our emotional space, the body is there to alert us, to let us know we must act.

If you don't listen to your body, the illness will become stronger and it can develop into cancer and other diseases. To practice healing your body and cleaning your space from any sickness or diseases, take the following coaching steps:

Homeplay:

1. Choose the part of your body you would like to heal. It can be a specific illness, or it can be any unusual pain.

2. What is the result you want to change? Write down your ideal outcome, be specific.

3. Connect to your Essence and to your heart. Close your eyes, call out and ask God (or your preferred deity), "Show me my root!"

4. Listen to the specific moment you experienced that caused the creation of the specific root. Write, describing the experience, what you saw, what you felt.

5. Close your eyes again. Listen and recall what meaning/ belief you created because of that experience. For example: "I am alone" or "no one loves me." Feel the parts of the body that are connected to your illness.

6. Acknowledge the impact. What have the impact and consequences been of having this belief in your life? Write the impact down.

7. Close your eyes and imagine that the specific part/parts of the body that is/are affected being separated from you in a way that you can see it in front of you. You can picture it on your bed or your couch, like a friend ready to have a conversation.

8. Listen to what your part of the body has to say about the cause of your illness.

9. Take responsibility for the part/parts of your body that is/are causing you to be ill or causing you pain. Ask for forgiveness and allow yourself to imagine the part replying to you and accepting your completion.

10. Picture hugging that part of your body and create an agreement with it. Recreate your relationship with it and give your word to take care of whatever root you found.

11. Imagine a pink and violet light surrounding you and the body part.

12. Picture the other parts of your body inviting the affected area to come back to the body.

13. Picture the part that was sick being healthy, celebrating with the other parts of your body.

14. Now celebrate! If you can dance or jump, do that. If you need to move your body, internally celebrate that you are healed.

15. Declare: I thank you, God, for healing me. I am in perfect health and my life is in perfect peace.

16. What actions will you take to keep the space in your body clear? Write the actions and names of people that you will clean up with in case it is necessary.

17. Share your breakthrough with as many people you can!

THE POWER OF ESSENCE VISUALIZATION

Visualization is done by our mind. It forms a mental image, picture, and specific result that you would like to manifest. Yes, the mind is a great tool that, in combination with the intention of our Essence, can create an extraordinary impact.

Visualization without Essence is not permanent. That is why the law of attraction by itself does not work. Many people get frustrated because they are visualizing and nothing is happening. The truth is that most of the time it is the Ego who is wanting something from visualization. The visualization is about an attachment of the Ego versus what God really wants for us. The mind is so powerful that it can bring you what you want, although in many cases it is not necessarily what you need.

Your Essence knows exactly what you need and really want. There's an infinite wisdom source within you, evolved enough to really know what's best in the manifestation of your *purpose* beyond what your Ego thinks is best.

My twins, Estevan and David, were born prematurely. I was looking forward to holding them in my arms. They were my first children and I was ready to become a mother. Everything with my pregnancy seemed to be progressing well until I went into labor when I was only thirty-two weeks along.

I had an emergency Cesarean section, and that is how the miracle of my twins' lives in the outside world began with me. They were so tiny and yet so perfect in my eyes. I couldn't hold them because they had to be immediately transferred into the neonatal intensive care unit (NICU).

They had needles and cables all around their little bodies. While I was happy to see my babies alive, I remained deeply worried. The first week for my newborns and my family was okay amid the emotional rollercoaster of their birth. My mother and their father were there with me, supporting me.

I don't know what I would have done if I had not had the love of my family surrounding me, because what came next was the most difficult and painful experience I had experienced as a mother.

The twins had only been alive seven days when one of them, Estevan, started having signs of a dangerous illness. Soon it was confirmed that he had necrotizing enterocolitis (NEC), a devastating disease that affects mostly the intestines of premature infants. The wall of the intestine is invaded by bacteria, which causes local infection and inflammation that can ultimately destroy the wall of the bowel (intestine). The exact cause of NEC wasn't known at that time.

Estevan's case was severe, and the doctor ordered a transfer from Elmhurst Hospital in Queens, New York, where he was born, to Mount Sinai in Manhattan where there was a specialized surgeon awaiting his arrival at the hospital.

I remember the ride there like it was yesterday. The ambulance ride between two hospitals, seeing him surrounded by a group of angels in the form of doctors and nurses, his little eyes looked like crystals. His eyes were crystalline like the eyes of someone who is dying because his life was slipping away.

When we finally arrived at the hospital the doctor looked at me directly in my eyes and asked, "Do you believe in God?"

"Yes," I replied.

"Please pray that what we find, we can fix."

There was no way to know where the bacteria had damaged his intestine. The bacteria usually will consume the intestines. Approximately 50 percent of babies who have NEC die from this condition.

"In very simple words," he explained, "we will open Estevan's belly with an incision from one side to the other, look for a hole in the intestine, and remove any dead or dying intestinal tissue."

I was confused, desperate, and in so much fear of losing him. Can you imagine hearing that news? It was as if my whole world fell apart and I had to depend on a doctor I did not know to help me keep it together. Then I felt in my heart a sensation of deep and abiding faith, because you can also feel faith.

When I choose to connect to God's love within me, my pain was transformed into hope. It was not just in the doctor's hands, it was in God's hands through the surgeon. I did something that has the most power to heal, to clean, to destroy the old, and to build the new. I surrendered.

As I surrendered to God's mercy, I instantly knew my son was going to be okay. I started visualizing with my heart and soul the future of my son, even though my mind was screaming that he was going to die. I went beyond the noise of my head and I dug into the power of God's love.

I pictured my son older—at five, ten, fifteen, twenty, thirty years, and even older. I saw him next to his brother David. Estevan was healthy, strong, and vibrant. I cried many tears; but, these were tears of faith. I kept visualizing nonstop and even when my body was tired and weak, my mind and my heart were strong. Then, I witnessed a miracle.

The surgery was scheduled to last seven hours; but, after only four hours, a nurse came out screaming, "It's a miracle, it's a miracle!"

I was told that medical personnel don't believe in miracles, but for sure, I was wrong. The bacteria only damaged his appendix and he wouldn't need it to live a healthy life. My son was saved.

When I look back at the experience, I can now genuinely say that I am deeply grateful for the most difficult moment of my life. Because of what I experienced with my twins, I know what comprises true faith because I now know the power of vision and visualization.

What is your miracle? What is it that may seem impossible to you right now? It can be your health or the health of someone you really love. It can be a dream that for your mind is never going to happen, but your soul will just know it is possible.

ACTIVE MEDITATION

Active meditation is a transformational tool that allows you to meditate while reading this book. I like to use a powerful meditation by Legacy coach Liz Stern. She is an extraordinary friend, coaching client, and business partner. She knows the importance of transformational active meditation to clear up our space, especially in times of pressure, distress, or challenge.

Creative Meditation

Close your eyes and take a breath in and out, three times. Release any tension in your face. Feel your muscles go limp as your breath leaves your body.

You don't need perfect attention. This doesn't require you to stop thoughts, allow them to flow. If you notice your mind wandering, gently bring it back to your breath. Enjoy this brief time of doing nothing as a gift to yourself. A gift of exploration and creativity for you to harness throughout your day.

When you are ready, get as comfortable as you can in a chair with your feet on the floor and your hands at your sides, or lie down with your arms at your sides. Let go of any unnecessary tension and allow your body and mind to relax. Close your eyes and breathe in and out. Breathe in for four seconds. Hold for four seconds. Breathe out for five seconds. Let's do this five times, together.

1. Breathe in for four seconds, hold for four seconds, and breathe out for five seconds.

2. Breathe in for four seconds, hold for four seconds, and breathe out for five seconds.

3. Breathe in for four seconds, hold for four seconds, and breathe out for five seconds.

4. Breathe in for four seconds, hold for four seconds, and breathe out for five seconds.

5. Breathe in for four seconds, hold for four seconds, and breathe out for five seconds.

Now let your breathing return to its natural state. Breathe in, breathe out.

Focus your mind on a place that you would like to go. Imagine a place you have always wanted to visit. You have not been to it before, yet you want to explore it.

Imagine you find yourself standing in the center of a plaza. What season is it where you are located? Is it sunny? Look at the streets and alleys and choose a direction to walk. What are the streets made of? Look at the buildings, are they familiar? The structures may or may not have been something you have seen. It is up to you.

What foods are people eating?

Take a breath, smell the air, and untangle all the smells.

Observe how the people are dressed.

As you begin your exploration, feel the energy of anticipation as you explore. This place is your own. Allow your mind to surprise you with each step. What do you see? This place is yours and yours alone, your mind creates it.

Enjoy the excitement that comes with exploration. Take in what you see, the people you meet, and how you feel. Feel the energy coursing through you as you wander. There is no need for expectations.

On this journey enjoy your experience and the time out of your usual daily activities while allowing your mind to create a reality that is one of pleasure for you.

Allow your mind to wander.

A chime will end the meditation in a few minutes. In the meantime, enjoy the opportunity to reflect on what you have seen and experienced. Reflect on the place your mind created for you to explore, what you have learned, and how the experience will feed your creativity in everyday life.

Now it is time for us to return to our day. Breathe and relax where you are and begin to wiggle your fingers and toes. Feel the energy within them and in your body as you become aware of yourself again. Everything around you is here for you to give you creative energy.

You are always able to return to this place within your mind's eye when you want to refresh that creative energy. You may find that a sound or smell will take you there as well and allow you to see with a new lens.

I love this meditation because when you clear up your space, creativity is possible, productivity is possible, transformation is possible.

DEATH

Many people tell me that even though it is challenging, they understand the concept of completion with people who are still here with us. What about people that have passed away? How can you heal the pain of losing someone you love? In this case, you have had a great relationship with this person, but you can't see how you can live without them.

If you carry the suffering of losing someone, your space is not complete. This feeling will consume the energy and your vibration will be affected by your feelings.

What I am about to share with you has the potential of clearing up your pain, and if you so choose, the suffering of death can disappear from your life.

I was practicing meditation many years ago in upstate New York at a beautiful place in Phoenicia. I remained still so I could hear my heartbeat. It was getting slower by the minute. There was a moment when the beats were so long in between that it felt like my heart completely stopped; I could not hear it for at least thirty minutes.

I was in a panic because I could not move my body at all. My mind was also quiet, and I could not hear it. What happened next was an event that transformed my relationship with life and death forever. I felt complete peace within me, I felt love, I felt the perfection of God. I felt it all and nothing at the same time. I understood through that meditation what I have learned in my studies. Death is only a transition of form.

If we are God in Essence, and through death our body is gone but our Essence remains, how can we die at all? God is eternal, so we are eternal. Why, you may ask, is death just an illusion of the mind? This is because only the Ego dies. The Ego fears death so much because it knows its power won't be eternal. Only the power of who we really are stays in the Universe forever.

When someone you know is no longer here, their transition only brings them closer to you because the limitation of time and space will no longer exist. Their Essence will be with you until you are in the same Essence with them.

Don't cry for the loss of them in your life because you haven't lost them. Cry to celebrate their life. Honor people in your life by manifesting your *purpose.* I am sure that if they were here, they would want you to be happy.

Angela had been suffering deeply the loss of her mother for over two years. She was unhappy, and nothing would fulfill her because her pain was bigger than any joy in her life. When she shared with me her experience through my coaching, she realized she was carrying her pain to honor her mother.

Today we are told that for us to be good kids, parents, brothers, and sisters, we must grieve, and that the longer we grieve, the more love we have for our loved one. Many people perceive that it is improper to recover quickly from the death of a loved one and continue with one's life. I asked Angela what her mother would want, to see her suffering because of her death, or to see her happy and enjoying life in her honor.

"To see me happy," she replied. She recognized that her Ego would make her feel guilty any time she was trying to be happy even for a moment. She was a "bad daughter" when she wasn't in pain over her loss.

She realized in this coaching that her mom was and would be forever with her, and she promised herself in front of hundreds of other people who were in tears, touched by her story, that she was going to allow joy into her life, fulfill her *purpose,* and share her gifts with the world in honor of her mother.

I invite you to honor those who left before you. The best way to do this is to live your best life. For all of you facing the death of a loved one, I dedicate to you the following beautiful poem:

LIVE IT

"All Is Well"

by Henry Scott Holland (1847–1918),
Canon of St Paul's Cathedral

Death is nothing at all,
I have only slipped into the next room
I am I and you are you
Whatever we were to each other, that we are still.
Call me by my old familiar name,
Speak to me in the easy way which you always used
Put no difference in your tone,
Wear no forced air of solemnity or sorrow
Laugh as we always laughed at the little jokes we enjoyed together.
Play, smile, think of me, pray for me.
Let my name be ever the household word that it always was,
Let it be spoken without effect, without the trace of shadow on it.
Life means all that it ever meant.
It is the same as it ever was, there is unbroken continuity.
Why should I be out of mind because I am out of sight?
I am waiting for you, for an interval, somewhere very near,
Just around the corner.
All is well.

CHAPTER 6

Now What?

ACTIONS = RESULTS

Now that you know your *purpose* and you have cleaned up your space to live it, your next step is to take massive action for its manifestation. Start first with the inner you; that is where the foundation of lasting results truly lies.

Motivation is not enough if there isn't a deep transformation in your life. This chapter will make you move your butt, not just to dance and celebrate, but to move you to the actions you know you must take in your Essence. Your Ego will try to sabotage your results at any cost! I will coach you on how to master your actions and have effective results in your life and business.

ESSENCE REMINDER

Without action there is no reaction.

VISION

Your vision determines your reality. What is the type of life you want to have? Vision comes from your Essence. Your vision is the manifestation that already exists in the eyes of God for you. God sees what we cannot see, and he translates this into our vision. Your vision is the *result* of you living your *purpose*. A *purpose* without vision or a vision without *purpose* does not exist.

Some people are afraid to create a compelling vision because they do not want to be disappointed. What they don't realize is that a true vision is larger than us, and even larger than what we can imagine. The vision that we consciously create is still only a pointer to the exceptional life that God or the Universe has for us. Dare to dream and to follow your inner vision. I guarantee you will be surprised when you start receiving much more than what you planned.

Plans are good, but you can't be attached to them or to anything else. Attachment to a result creates suffering, and suffering creates disconnection from your inner God. Create, plan, and let go. How do you do that?

Take the following steps:

- Pray, mediate, and connect in silence with your heart and ask God, "What is the vision You have for me? What is next? What is Your vision in my life? I trust You more than I trust myself, because only through trusting You can I truly trust myself."

- Let the message come to you. You may see pictures or results in the form of a movie. Stay still and enjoy the projection of your future.

PURPOSE

- In quantum physics, there are multiple possibilities of realities and you can choose from them. In those possibilities the vision of your *purpose* is clear, and it is the biggest of all. If you are reading this book you are destined for greatness and this vision will be revealed to you.

- Write down your vision in detail from what is in your heart, starting backwards like this:

    a. What is the legacy you want to leave behind when you leave the physical form? Include what will continue living when you transition. Example: foundations, organizations, companies, family. Make sure that in the description of the vision of your *purpose* you include your non-profit side and your for-profit side. It is essential to include both.

    b. Where do you see yourself in twenty years? Describe the results in your relationship with loved ones, friends, and the world. Describe in detail your results in business. The business you described in your vision must be connected to your *purpose*—exactly what you would do if you had all the money in the world!

    c. Where do you see yourself in ten years? (Follow B format)

    d. Where do you see yourself and your *purpose* in five years? (Follow B format)

e. Where do you see yourself and your *purpose* in one year? (Follow B format)

f. Where do you see yourself and your *purpose* in six months? (Follow B format)

g. What is your ninety-day vision for yourself and your *purpose?* (Follow B format)

90 DAY VISION GAME

Once you have a transformational, compelling vision you will now bring it all together into the present. You can easily recognize if that is what you are doing right now with your time. Ask yourself: Is what I am doing taking me closer to my vision or it is a distraction? The best way to know if you are on the right path for your vision is to create a measurable game. I call it a game because I like to compare our vision to sports.

To win you must be on the court and not sitting down watching from the bench. You must play full out, work with your team, keep the integrity of your game, follow the rules, score, and celebrate!

LET'S CREATE YOUR GAME

Homeplay:

This game will include your inner game and outer game.

- Inner game: Who you will *be*, who you will become, what is your evolution, what is your consciousness, your awareness, the development of your inner self, your spiritual self, your health?

- Outer Game: financial results, relationship results.

1. Write down what specific result you would like to accomplish in ninety days with your inner game and outer game. Include all areas: spirituality, health, relationships, and finances.

2. Write down where you must be in sixty days, including all areas, to accomplish your results in ninety days.

3. Write down where you must be in thirty days including all areas to accomplish your results in ninety days.

4. Write two actions per week that you will take for each result of each area in the first four weeks. Include specific dates and schedule them in your calendar.

5. Start playing and honor your word. You must have an impeccable relationship with your word and clean up with yourself when not honoring it.

6. You can adjust your actions in accordance with your results each week. Play full out and be flexible to change things according to the signs of the Universe.

Once you get to your first thirty-day milestone, create the actions for the next four weeks and do the same for the last four weeks up to the ninety-day mark.

ESSENCE REMINDER

When playing your game, celebrate each result. Find accountability with people who have higher standards. Get a coach and be coachable. Play full out. Don't give excuses.

Just be it and do it!

SPIRITUAL RELATIONSHIP WITH MONEY

Many people feel discomfort when creating a financial vision and playing the game of money, especially those who consider themselves spiritual and those who don't put money over other things. I know this because in coaching thousands of people I have found many leaders who are great at making money in something that is not their *purpose*, but as soon as they start following their dreams they end up broke!

Regarding my own personal story around money, I went from being completely broke for the first four years of living my *purpose* to making my first million dollars in less than three months of healing my relationship with money. While learning from my friend and mentor Gary, I identified my own limiting beliefs around my relationship with money.

I used to say things like, "I don't care about money," "I just want to serve," and "Money is not really that important to me." I attended many personal development seminars about money mindset and I even declared "I have a millionaire mind." I was right! In my Essence, I was a millionaire, but in my mind, I wasn't buying it.

I was separating God and money. Spirituality and business were two different things for me. I learned that if I didn't see God in *everything*, I didn't see Him at all. This includes money, of course. It was comforting for me to think about money as any form of spirituality. I learned that money was created to compensate us for our *purpose. Mic drop!* What? If I rejected money with my thoughts, words, or actions, I was telling God no thank you, I don't want your compensation.

What many people think of as being humble for rejecting money is the highest form of arrogance by rejecting God's gift to you. Reflect on that. How many times has a person tried to help you and you said no, even though you needed the help? Right there, you are rejecting God.

How many times have you allowed others to underpay you, steal from you, or take advantage of you when you knew in your heart it was wrong? You rejected God's advice right there. How many times have you refused to get paid because you felt it was dishonorable to accept money for doing what you love?

You said, "No, no, no, and again no" to God. Repeatedly. Stop feeling badly. I just want you to see the impact of your actions and recreate your relationship with money. Money is energy, energy is everywhere, and God is within everything. It is only when you use money from your Ego that you are misusing the intention behind the creation of money.

ESSENCE REMINDER

Money only makes you more of who you are,
Essence or Ego.

MONEY PRINCIPLES

Here are five top money principles that will empower you to grow and keep a healthy and powerful money tree:

1. Giving back: There is no such a thing as too small a contribution when giving back. The ideal situation is to donate a minimum of 10 percent of every dollar you make to a charity or charities of your choice. Even if it is less than that, do it every week until you can give 10 percent. The secret to receiving is giving! Some people will say, "how can I give back when what I have is not enough to cover my own expenses?" Well, you do not have enough because you are not giving enough.

2. Saving is a must: Not matter how much you earn, it is essential that you save, you must save at least 10 percent of your income. "Do not save what is left after spending, but spend what is left after saving."—Warren Buffett

3. Tracking your money: You *must* know how much money is coming in, going out, when, where, and how. Clarity is power! Tracking your money is honoring it. This means you are grateful for each dollar God provides and that you are ready to open space for more. There are many money tracking systems. You can start with a pen and paper, QuickBooks, or even more sophisticated systems. No matter how you do it, until you are managing what you have now correctly, the Universe will not give you more.

4. Learn every day: Your money tree will grow as much as you do. No matter how successful you already are, there is always space to learn more and you *must*. The Ego likes to be in its comfort zone; especially when you have accomplished a certain level of success. Do not allow it to fool you. The key is to surround yourself with people who have the results you admire and are manifesting. There is so much great information out there, whether free or for a fee, that will continue elevating your consciousness and your spiritual relationship with money.

5. Focus on your *purpose*: Ask yourself why you are manifesting more money. The Universe won't give you what you want; rather, it will give you what you *need* to fulfill your destiny. It is crucial, and a human need for people to find and live their life's *purpose*. Once you understand that financial abundance is merely a vehicle to serve your mission, and it is your mission,

not your money that will fulfill your heart, you will be free to focus on living your legacy every day of your life. Focus on how many people you can serve doing what you love, and the money will follow you naturally. This is a universal law.

FIND THE ROOT OF AN UNHEALTHY RELATIONSHIP WITH MONEY

Homeplay:

Find the root cause of a result with money that you'd like to shift:

1. What is the result you want to change? Close your eyes breathe three times in and out with your hands facing up. Write it down. Include how long this has been happening.

2. Connect to your Essence and to your heart. Call out and ask, "Show me my root belief."

3. Listen and see the specific moment that caused you to create the specific root belief you have against money. Examples: You heard your mom or dad complain about money, family fighting over money, not having enough money, having more money than others and feeling guilty about it.

4. Close your eyes again and listen to the declaration of the Ego. What did your Ego tell you about money? Write

it down, for this is your root belief. Examples: Money is bad, I hate money, money is never enough, money is evil, money makes people greedy.

5. Acknowledge the impact. What has been the impact of having this root belief in your life? Write down the consequences of this root belief in your life.

6. Take responsibility. Declare "I am responsible!"

7. Are you willing to change it? Say "I choose to transform my spiritual relationship with money *now*."

8. Go back to that crucial moment, listen to what your Essence says to you. Close your eyes.

9. What is the Essence/God declaration? God has always been with you, including then. God was speaking to you and was sharing with you the true meaning of that experience. What did God say? What was the affirmation? Example: "God is love—money is love," "Money is a blessing," "God is in money and money is within me," "God, money, and I are one."

10. Which one do you choose? The declaration of the Ego or the Essence? Write it down.

11. Share your results with those you love and care about.

DOING BUSINESS FROM ESSENCE

1. You must choose where and with whom you share your presence. You must see your business and presence as a privilege. Who are you sharing your time and business with? Ask yourself, "Is this person/event bringing value to my business/life? Can I add value to this person/company?" You are selecting someone who will be a shareholder in your life. Wherever you go you must ask yourself "Am I giving value? Am I receiving value?" The answer must always be *yes*.

2. You must be responsible for whatever happens to your brand wherever you go and who you are being at all times. You are also taking responsibility for your state of being. Make sure you are grounded.

3. Your Essence will know who is in alliance with you. Ask God "Who do you want me to meet?"

4. Your Essence will send you where you are destined to be. The Universe is always in alignment, and it is always responding.

5. Don't be afraid to let go of a client. The right people will come to you.

6. The right client recognizes your value and honors your services.

7. Your circumstances don't matter, because the priority must be to provide value and live your *purpose* no matter what.

8. Honor your brand. You never know where the next connection will come from. You must be congruent wherever you are, wherever you go. Your business will reflect this.

9. You need to be present so everything will align to your presence.

10. Be impeccable and honor your word.

11. Raise your standards.

12. Today and the now is all we have, nothing is guaranteed.

13. Always over-deliver.

14. You're part of history, you've paid your dues, now it's time for you to collect what you've been planting all these years. It is your time. Own it.

ESSENCE REMINDER

By being your authentic self, you will never have competition. Competition only happens when you are trying to be someone you are not. When you're being yourself there is no competition because in the world there is no one like you.

Once, on a business trip, I thought I was going to die on the plane due to heavy turbulence. I thought, *I can die in peace, and I can leave knowing I lived my purpose, my life, and I can leave my kids and family set.* My friend Les Brown says, "Live full and die empty. Don't take your gifts to your grave." It's up to you to shine, to honor your *purpose* and your family, because we don't know when our last day will be. It is up to you to make a shift.

WHAT ABOUT YOUR WORD WHEN WORKING AS A TEAM?

Integrity in both personal and professional endeavors is not negotiable. We must accept when we have made a mistake and recreate a new commitment. We must see the person and have a conversation. Acknowledge when we are not being congruent and make a new commitment.

I previously recommended the extraordinary book *The Power of Now* by Eckhart Tolle. He tells us that we will be unconscious and judgmental at times. Anytime we are conscious of our unconsciousness or in our Ego, we are like a big eye observing ourselves, and we are enlightened.

Enlightened people are not always free of their Ego, they are just aware of it and don't act on it. And if they do act on it, they clean up.

This is what we practice in our group coaching. If participants are one minute late for a session or for an assignment and they didn't communicate beforehand, then the participant must clean up. Accountability means saying, "I take responsibility for being late and I commit to being on time from now on. No excuses." Recommit to clean up the space. It takes courage and commitment to keep space clean. If you don't clean up, your team, business, or company is affected by that energy.

We are not blaming others for our circumstances and we are not excusing ourselves. It is vital that we take full ownership. There is an impact when we don't honor our word. No guilt. The Ego wants to avoid responsibility by feeling guilty. Guilt is a way of avoiding responsibility. I understand my actions have an impact on people, the world, and my *purpose*. I get it, and I am committed to honoring my word. Although we think as individuals, we win the game as a team. The significant things in life are created by a team.

Get used to declaring: "I am taking responsibility. I am cleaning up my sh—!" (By which I mean the stronger version of *poopoo*!) Part of the responsibility of being a leader means expressing when you are not feeling right or excellent. When I don't feel right, I let people know. Give yourself permission to inform others when you are not feeling right when working with them. It is an invitation to be vulnerable. Share when you don't feel right or are feeling confronted. Leaders invite others to connect to us and do not take people or their lives for granted.

Some people take their lives because they don't think they matter. I've had family members who have committed suicide. Although we don't control what people do, we can be the difference whether people live or die. We acknowledge and honor our darkness; however, light is stronger than darkness.

Light equals the heart and Essence, or Light = heart/ Essence. Let's be vulnerable with who we are in all aspects and give ourselves permission to shine and remind each other of how beautiful and extraordinary we are by being each other's mirrors—a true reflection of greatness. I want to make sure that I bring you the Essence of action.

Action from Essence is fun. When you are living your *purpose*, you really do not work a day in your life. I am grateful that I get paid for doing what I love, and this is a feeling that I am committed to bring to every person I meet.

You deserve a life of fulfillment, and when you act to manifest what is in your heart, the quality of your life is shifted forever. You are here to see with your own eyes the manifestation of your *purpose* and to live a legacy that will continue impacting the world beyond your time on this planet.

The world needs your gifts. Your contribution is essential and so is your vision! The more you manifest your *purpose,* the more people who need it will cross your path. They are lost and looking for you! When you take the Essence actions, you bring what is invisible to the mind's eye to become visible by the heart of humanity. Have fun with your vision and your plans. Manifest the abundance that God has in store for you through your *purpose*!

PART III

SHARE IT

Your *purpose* comes alive when you share it with the world. When you share your God-given gifts, there is a piece of your soul in everyone who receives your gift. You can only share your *purpose* when you are in front, shining your light.

Yet the spiritual Ego loves to hide. Being shy is one of the multiple ways the Ego tries to use as an excuse for not taking responsibility for your greatness. Similarly, people may think that by not making too much noise and staying quiet, they are doing a good thing for themselves and for others. The Ego hates being judged. It prefers to stay safely in the corner and in a comfort zone, so it won't shake things up too much.

How do we learn to shine our light if we have been told by society not to be conceited? We often hear things like: "Please don't think that you are all that great."

I challenge that ideology. Why not think that? I *know* that you *are* all that. You are God and there isn't anything bigger than God. You are all that because your Essence is part of it all. It is the Ego's arrogance that will cause you to think you are not.

ESSENCE REMINDER

Own your light, your greatness, and your God-given power to create, manifest, and transform the world.

CHAPTER 7

Coming Out of the Spiritual Closet

I encourage you to read one of my favorite poems *"Our Deepest Fear,"* by Marianne Williamson. The powerful words of the poem were quoted by Nelson Mandela in one of his empowering speeches. The words represent the mind's struggle for accepting one's greatness. I have many great and powerful mentors in my life, people whose wisdom I have been blessed to learn from. Despite all the mentors I have been fortunate to have in my life, one of the most powerful messages in overcoming adversity came from one of the very first, my mother. She could make a positive impact in the world, and especially in my world, regardless of her circumstances.

I witnessed how my mother one day decided to start her own business as a beauty product salesperson. She is intelligent, hardworking, has a quick mind, and loves to read. She would frequently purchase books about business and sales, read these books, and share them with us.

It was through my mother's inspiring business methods that I became so passionate about books. My mom's passion led her to grow her business to the point she had over two hundred women on her team.

She would meet her clients door-to-door while still inspiring strong business women from her team, including the low revenue leaders.

Although some people closed the door in my mother's face, she didn't give up. She eventually discovered that other people would open the doors of their homes and hearts to her. I saw my mom become a star, and she reflected what she was promoting. She became an independent, strong woman.

What I loved about my mother's work ethic the most was that the more success she achieved, the humbler and more giving she became. She would invest time and energy into training the women. She loved helping them succeed, but it was her greatest joy to see them transform into powerful stars as well.

My mom received multiple awards for her accomplishments. She traveled the world and she earned a lot of money. From her I learned the value of humanitarian work. Together, we fed the homeless. Even though we had a housekeeper, she always treated her like a member of our family. She would have her meals with us, vacation with us—she was a part of our family dynamic and part of our everyday life.

My mom is admired and loved by so many people. She taught me to smile wherever I go, to ask servers for their names, and to always say please and thank you. She instilled in me the importance of being present with people. She taught me to look directly in their eyes and make them feel special. She also taught me there is always time to be gracious and kind to others. Because of her, I now understand that when some people may appear to be mean towards others, it may simply be the individual's inner child crying because they are stressed or in pain.

When I found my *purpose*, my mom found hers. When I healed my past, she healed hers. When I became a coach, she became a coach as well. When I doubted myself, she was there to shine her light and show me mine. God will always bring the right angels for you to grow and fulfill your destiny. Once you accept that you are divine, you are out of the spiritual closet created by the collective Ego that wants to keep us all trapped. It is for this reason many unconscious people use religion, personal, and spiritual growth to manipulate others.

When I started being a coach, I would dress differently. I tried to fit other people's concept of a coach. If I was in a spiritual retreat, I felt too materialistic. If I was in a business seminar, I felt too spiritual.

One night after a networking event, I felt so alone, and didn't understand why I didn't want to be there. Everyone was drinking and not paying attention to what other people were really saying. These Hollywood-type people were so into themselves and their Ego I felt there was no one home.

My mom is admired and loved by so many people. My mom taught me that there is always time to be kind to others. She taught me to smile wherever I go, to ask servers for their name, to always say please and thank you, and to look at people in their eyes and make them feel special. I learned from her that what appears to be mean on the outside is just people's inner child crying from being stressed or in pain.

It is from my mother I learned the value of humanitarian work. Together, we fed the homeless. Even though we had a housekeeper, she always treated her like a member of our family. She would have her meals with us, vacationing with—she was a part of a family dynamic and a part of our normal life. Because of her large heart, my mom has received multiple awards for her accomplishments. She could travel the world and she earned a lot of money.

When I found my *purpose*, my mom found hers. When I healed my past, she did also. When I became a coach, she did as well. When I doubt myself, she was there to shine her light and show me mine. God will always bring the right angels for you to grow and fulfill your destiny. You just must let God bring them to you.

Once you accept you are divine you are out of the spiritual closet. This closet is created by the collective Ego that wants to keep us all trap. Therefore, many unconscious people use religion or event personal and spiritual growth to manipulate others.

I remember when I started being a coach, I would dress differently, and I tried to fit other people's concept of a coach. If I was in a spiritual retreat I felt to materialistic, if I was in a business seminar, I felt too spiritual.

One night after being in a networking event, everyone was drinking and not even paying attention of what people were saying. In Hollywood, many people are focused on their Ego and themselves. felt so alone and I didn't understand why I was there. I truly didn't want to be there.

When I got home, I was so upset. My mom said, "Karen, you have two options. Go and live on a mountain or transform everyone who comes around you."

You already know my choice. My Ego wanted to convince me that I didn't belong there, that "others" were too shallow. It was my own spiritual Ego trying to separate me from others and my *purpose*, because the Ego loves separation, and of course it loves to be right.

I learned to use the shining light of Carmen, my Ego, to open the doors of glamourous events, attend red carpet events, and be the center of attention. As Carmen, I could speak some people's language. Once I had their attention, my Essence would speak and their hearts would awaken.

Carmen and Karen are a perfect combination. In general, Ego keeps us in the closet because it doesn't know that outside of it there is a role for it as well! Your Ego and Essence can work as a team. When you dance this dance in harmony, you have captured the beauty of being human.

A great way to dance between mind and Essence and create a healthy relationship is by doing declarations. I love them so much that I use them before I start any training. The definition of a *declaration* is "to state an official intention to undertake a particular course of action or adopt a particular status." A declaration has the power of intention behind it. Affirmations, on the other hand, can sound similar, but the impact is more on a superficial level. Being positive alone is not enough.

If you don't mean what you declare from your Essence, what you are saying will become simply motivation and not transformative. This book is about the core, and for me the core is going deep to ensure lasting change. I learned to be hyperaware of my language, my vibration, and my energy.

When you ask people "How are you?" and they reply "Fine," they are not fine. They are saying, "I don't want you to know that I am feeling miserable," or simply, "I don't give a crap about who is asking." In either case, the Ego is hiding in the closet of being "fine." I sometimes want to yank them out by their hair, and then I remember that I am not my violent Ego and I change my approach.

ESSENCE REMINDER

Your words from Essence have power. Your Essence words are seeds that when planted in the soil of your life will produce the fruits of your results.

Homeplay:

Stand up in front of the mirror and read these declarations out loud. Yes, I said *out loud*, and don't cheat, my Essence is watching you. You will receive bonus points if you say them with my Colombian accent!

Declarations for Success

- I am *happy*!
- I am my *purpose*!
- I am *passion*!
- I am *light*!
- I am *sexy*, and I *know it*! (Repeat this one)
- I am *fun*!
- I am *abundance*!
- I am *connected* to *source*!
- I am *love*!
- I *honor* my *gifts*!
- I *share* my *legacy*!
- I *transform* the *world*!
- I am a *shining star*!

THE POWER OF WORDS OF GRATITUDE IN YOUR BUSINESS

While training other entrepreneurs into building *purpose*-transformational leadership businesses, I share the following gratitude statements to move them into the direction of their Essence's vision. I invite you to read with your heart open and let God guide you into your next step.

God, thank You for the opportunity and the privilege of service. I am grateful for all our past individual challenges that make us ready for this journey. I accept that I can't control many things, but I can choose how I face and respond to every one of those challenges.

We leave the need to control knowledge as we find the access to our wisdom. We put our hearts, voices, heads, beings, our life—everything in Your hands so You can guide us. We put our business in Your hands. With all the tools we develop, we can take our business to the next level. We are ready to grow personally and in our business. We are ready to leave a legacy behind. We are ready to be the best version of ourselves. We are ready to recognize when we are not being our best version, and we are ready to take full responsibility for it. We will learn to jump into the unknown and transform our lives, and to jump out of our comfort zone.

We are ready to contribute to our team. We are ready to receive wisdom, health, and abundance that You have for us in our transformational business and life. Thank You for the technology to facilitate and to connect. Thank You for our time, the investment of our energy and money, and our commitment so we can fulfill our *purpose*. Thank You for the ability to choose our mission and we are ready to see with Your eyes. We dedicate to You this amazing adventure and journey. Thank You in advance for all the blessings we will receive.

We trust this process. We are flexible, committed to taking action, honoring our word, giving our word, and giving the best of ourselves. We are here to fully serve.

We are ready. We are ready. *We are ready!*

Thank You God, today and always.

Namaste.

I love to end a prayer, meditation, gratitude statement, and more with the word *Namaste* for its spiritual definition that you can read below.

ESSENCE REMINDER

Namaste: I honor the place in you in which the entire Universe dwells. I honor the place in you which is of love, of truth, of light, and of peace. When you are in that place in you, and I am in that place in me, we are one.

A CONVERSATION ABOUT FEAR

Most people don't want to get out of their spiritual closet because they are afraid of the unknown. Fear can cause triggers that may cause a person to fall back into old habits because of a lack of consistency. When one isn't living one's *purpose* fully, the Ego gets scared. It knows that change comes from Essence.

You have the tools to make a transition in your life and business. It may not happen overnight, but you know what steps to take to seek out the *how.* In whatever you do, add the sharing of your wisdom and knowledge. It is very fulfilling. Replace fear by understanding where it comes from, then create clarity. Next, exchange fear for urgency to act. These tools apply to everyone.

Whenever the Ego brings confusion, fear, or the sense of being overwhelmed into your life, it is caused by a lack of clarity. We respond to our Ego by saying, "Thank you for reminding me: My life is my *purpose*, my *purpose* is my business!"

In the manifestation of our *purpose*, we get stronger by taking action despite our fear. This occurs by understanding where fear comes from. Transform fear by motivation, inspiration, and drive. What's on the other side of the manifestation of your *purpose* is extraordinary. However, to get there, there is always a fight between the Ego and Essence.

One powerful tool that I use to face, embrace, and transform fear are mantras. A *mantra* is a word or a sacred group of words, usually in Sanskrit, believed by teachers, students, and masters to have psychological and spiritual powers. Mantra meditation helps to go deeper into a state of consciousness. The earliest mantras were composed by Hindus in India and are at least three thousand years old.

My favorite one is the Devi Prayer. This is a prayer in honor of Kali, the goddess of transformation. You can use the mantra to create a powerful space for transformation:

> *"Kali is the goddess of transformation in Hinduism. She cut the head off the Ego and licked the blood of the Ego away with her tongue—a symbolic form of cleaning. She's aggressive in many ways, but also kind and loving.*

This duality represents the only way to create something new: by creating it from scratch."

- Let go of everything not in alignment that doesn't work for us to receive what God has for us. Sometimes transformation is painful and uncomfortable, but at same time fulfilling with a sense of peace, knowing what we do is right. Her sword represents higher knowledge for killing the Ego. Kali is strong and loving.

The Ego likes to keep everything the same. When coming out of the spiritual closet, the Ego will inevitably face Kali at any point when going deeper into your transformation. You will no longer tolerate the mediocrity of your Ego, nor will you buy into other people's.

When you are out of your spiritual closet, you raise your standards. You have no other choice than to be great. When you are out of the closet fully, the door is closed and there is no going back. You won't be able to undo your transformation. You are it, you know you are it, and your only way is to embrace your *purpose*.

IT'S UP TO YOU

It is your choice. You don't have to do this. You don't have to have an extraordinary life, you don't have to live your *purpose*, you don't have to shine. You now know what is to be in the dark side, and it is up to you to choose.

In life, the people who are choosing to transform the world aren't just giving exactly what they're supposed to give. They are willing to give more. People who are meant to succeed stay there. Going up is easy if you have what it takes, but to sustain that success takes an extra mile.

Once you make the choice to come out, the Universe will know you are ready. The only path is forward. You will still face challenges, of course, but the Universe will be in your favor. You will become what my spiritual Ego likes to call *one of God's favorite children.*

YOUR *PURPOSE* IN YOUR BUSINESS

As I healed my relationship with money, I learned to own my light. I also learned to embrace that I am a phenomenal businesswoman. One of the many benefits of being out of the spiritual closet is that you are no longer afraid to succeed, you are no longer afraid to be judged because you know it is going to happen anyway.

Some people don't like me because I teach sales and spirituality. In fact, I have a training that is called God Knows How to Sell. This program was controversial at the time it was first released. Many people thought I was using God to sell. Yes, that is true, I must confess, because everything I do in my business is done by God through me. God brings me perfect clients, the perfect partners, the perfect ideas, and even perfect readers like you!

As I have boldly built a multimillion-dollar business by applying the principles that I teach, it has become clearer to me that I must support those Essence leaders who are really making a difference and who are committed to make the world a better place.

The translation of manifestation in a *purpose*-filled business equates to and means sales. The word *sales* is a beautiful word that's been misused by multiple Egos. These Egos organize manipulation plans to make people buy things that they don't need or want.

Yet beyond the intentions of the Ego, there is the intention of the Essence and those who deserve to be transformed by *purpose*-driven results. By living your life's *purpose*, I teach you to build your empire for both nonprofit and for-profit organizations. This is because ultimately, the more sales you have, the more people you can serve.

SALES FROM ESSENCE VS. EGO

Make sure what you're selling is contributing to your *purpose*. There is no true sale if the only reason you are selling is for money. Money is the compensation for your gifts. Money is essential in a sale because there is no sale without it. If the reason you have in your head for your sales is coming from you, know that if it is not coming from your heart to build your *purpose*, or expand it, then it will not be an Essence sale. If you are only selling for money, even if you make great sales, they won't last. It will be momentary, and it will not grow with you.

You must be your product. You must breathe it, love it, and it must be part of yourself. Enjoy it. Your passion will go beyond your facts and numbers, and it will open the space for someone who wants to invest in you.

You must be passionate about your productivity. It is essential that you love it as much as you can, because other people will feel it. Even if you are not selling it directly, you must be so inspired by your product that your team will feel it. They will connect to that passion as well.

I say this again and again: Always *overdeliver*. Give more than what people expect. If this is what God wants to do with us, we must model it in our business.

Homeplay:

- Write down five inner aspects of your ideal client, either an individual or company, and include their values and their *purpose*.

- Write five outer characteristics of your ideal client, either an individual or company. Include demographics, facts, information, and details about them.

- Give value for free. Don't be afraid to give. Within your *purpose,* you can always find resources to share continually. This applies both in your personal life and in business.

- Come from the heart, come from a place of service, of contribution, and because you are ready, people will come to you.

- You're loving people when you are selling them something that will change their life, contribute to their entertainment, make them happier, and bring them joy.

SHARE IT

- Sales are a way for you to love your clients.
- Sales = love = fun.
- Whatever the Ego says, the reality is when you are selling, it is an act of love.
- When you are selling your *purpose*, it is an act of love.
- When you sell in Essence, there is no guilt in Essence sales, there is gratitude on both ends.
- When people invest in your company, give you money in exchange for your gift, and that sale comes from Essence, what is left for them is pure gratitude. What is possible after that is gratitude and more happy clients. They will talk about you and they will share about you.
- Your number one focus in business is for sales to come from Essence. This means integrity in service. Your client is first.
- When you acknowledge someone while selling, be authentic and their heart will open because your heart is open.
- People are not accustomed to being *seen*. When you listen to their story, find aspects of them you can acknowledge.
- Always ask them for permission to share your story.

- Include your most difficult story and your most challenging times, so they can really connect. They will feel they can relate. Your story has an impact, so keep sharing it.
- They need to see the impact of not having you, so they can appreciate you.
- Always thank your clients for their time, trust, and business.
- Essence sale is always effective.
- Essence sales you never lose; you always gain something on both sides. It will be a win-win all the way.
- Acknowledgment, acknowledgement, acknowledgment! This is the food of the heart.

THERE ARE THREE STAGES IN ESSENCE SALES

Stage 1

1. Whatever you sell must be connected to your *purpose.*
2. You must be your product.
3. You must be sure you are coming from a place of integrity. *Overdeliver!*
4. Make sure you have a support system in place so you can be ahead of the game and your growth for the next

phase. Identify and list your team who is ready for you and will serve. Always plan ahead!

5. Know the inner and outer aspects of your ideal client.

Stage 2

1. You don't make the sale; the sale comes to you. The sale is love.

2. Your sales are an act of love.

3. Manifestation of the sale.

    a. You ask permission to begin.

    b. Ask them to share their story, and listen to them intently.

    c. Authentically acknowledge your client from Essence.

    d. Ask permission to share your story.

    e. Deliver your story in a short manner, make sure you share your most difficult challenge and the bridge to your product and service.

    f. Receive their acknowledgement.

    g. Have client clarify their vision, ask questions like: Where are you going? What is your vision? What would you like to accomplish?

h. What is the challenge in the way of accomplishing their vision?

i. The *queen* of the sale: Tell them "This is exactly what we do!"

j. Let them know the impact of not fixing the problem; that they are letting go.

k. Ask and listen for the answer. "How much longer do you want to continue this? Do not wait anymore, the time is now!"

l. Ask permission to give options to solutions in any challenges.

m. Share the solutions in a clear way, make sure you include name and description of product, its regular price, and its special price.

n. Ask which option the client desires to take today.

o. Process the client's payment.

p. Follow up immediately. Give a heartfelt acknowledgement. Always thank your client.

Stage 3

Revisit with your client, reconnect, and keep them in your family. Always connect with your client beyond what they need.

IMPORTANT NOTE

Use this in every area of your life. These tools are perfect elements for your own consciousness and evolution. You are beautiful, you have been *seen*. We are grateful for you, and know that whatever you are going through it is part of a perfect plan. We can both heal and take action at the same time. I care about you, you are in my heart, and I believe in you.

THE NEXT STEPS

How do you know when it is time for the next step? The next step falls in front of me, as I am obedient with the calling that is within me. I am obedient to that vision and I am focused. I am obedient and surrender to my own calling. My calling and my *purpose* are bigger than me, bigger than the *purpose* in my head, and bigger than my business. As I surrender, I realize that within my plan there is always space for the surprise God has for me. As we allow God to show us the next step, we grow and get prepared.

ESSENCE REMINDER

There is always space for God's plan.

It is what we cannot see with our eyes that moves us to new heights to create a bigger impact. This inspires us to create extraordinary results, products, and services. These items make an even bigger impact due to the unseen magic that happens.

It is in what we cannot see and sometimes cannot understand consciously that the manifestation of God comes from.

As we move forward, all we dream of just takes faith; an extraordinary faith. You are the one to change the world, and as you accept this, you don't need to make it happen, you don't need to look for the answers. As you accept and surrender to this realization, you will find every answer you need within you.

The best coach is the one within your soul. Your best guide is within your Essence. As you listen to that voice and surrender, don't question what your soul is saying to you. Create all the breakthroughs you need and manifest all the amazing things you have in your life.

You will bring forward the ideal relationships, experiences, clients, investors, and partners when you trust your soul more than anyone and anything. As you trust that you are trusting God within you, as you are God, you can recognize the right people for the right opportunity.

ESSENCE REMINDER

You will manifest exactly what you need. The Universe and you are one.

ESSENCE Q & A

As you move forward into building your *purpose*-driven empire, let me give you access to some of the private transformational questions I have responded to in my coaching sessions. I have never shard this before this book. Know that you are special, and I am here for you. This is one of the ways I will overdeliver to you. As you see, I eat my own cookie, what I teach, I do. Below, please find examples of questions and answers that drive to the core of transformational business coaching.

Joe

Q1: What are five things I should do to build my *purpose*-driven business?

- Be clear of what makes you unique in your contribution to the world.
- Make sure the people who work with you, edify you.
- Make sure you yourself edify the people who have contributed to your success.
- Be present in what you share in social media, the content should bring value.
- Be present of the quality of what you are sharing.

Q2: What do you recommend as a morning routine to start each business day?

- Start and end the day with mantras.
- Have and use a gratitude list.
- Schedule everything on your calendar.
- Revive resources wherever you go.

- Share about your *purpose* every day.
- Don't let a day pass without touching a life for good.

Ljubo

Q1: How do we present our grand vision to others?

- Be clear with the *purpose* of your vision and make sure it is honoring your life's *purpose* and not your Ego's desires.
- Look at the manifestation of your vision as an emergency. Act as if it were life or death.
- Be prepared in both Essence and mind knowledge.
- If you're not growing with your vision, you're dying.
- Have a strategic plan of action with dates and times on a calendar.

Q2: What are the steps for an effective presentation of my life's *purpose* in business?

- Before you present, make sure people are connected to you.
- Declare: God, you speak to me, you talk through me.
- Acknowledge people. Thank them and honor them for their time.
- When you are presenting, always start with the three-minute story about yourself.
- Then begin your business presentation

    a. What is the product?

b. Why is it important?

c. What is the challenge?

d. Where are you going?

e. What do you need? How much do you know you need?

Nicholas

Q1: I've had a series of events in the past couple of months which I call "near misses." I get a call from a production company, they express their interest in my services, I send my material, and it doesn't materialize. What should I revise as a person and as a brand?

- Search for any traces of attachment of the outcome (Ego, doubting, fear).
- Tell the Ego "thank you for sharing."
- Your Essence will tell you if it is the right place to send your material.
- You will be in peace.
- You should be grateful if something doesn't align as you wished, for something else is in store for you, something greater.

Q2: You mentioned that you don't look for the sale or the client, they come looking for you. Could you please elaborate on that and how it may relate to my previous question?

- I became the ideal partner before I attracted it.
- Like the journey of finding the love of your life.
- As soon as I find myself having to push or trying to convince someone, I know that person is not right for me.
- Don't focus on convincing people who are not ready for you.
- Always create your intention.
- Be clear on what you're looking for professionally and personally.
- The right client will jump to it.

Marcela

Q1: My business is a nonprofit organization, how much money will I need to start?

- Your *business* is not a nonprofit organization.
- You have a business and you have a nonprofit.
- You cannot build profit off a nonprofit.
- Build your business first, then create your nonprofit.

- Your focus should initially be your business. Start donating 10 percent of your profit right away.

Q2: How to connect different products/services to my main *purpose*?

- If you serve many masters, you end up not serving anyone.
- Choose what you will focus on, so you can become a master.
- Focus on all the value you have to offer.

Victor

Q1: Now I'm surrounded by wealthy and influential people, but I still struggle with money issues. I feel I am still not as evolved as they are, but I know they trust me. These people want me as a friend and as a professional alliance. How can I cope with feeling inferior?

- The fact these people want to work with you shows that you both are on the same vibration. You are equal to them, you are just catching up.
- Your Ego will try to fight this and convince you that you are not enough and for the Ego, you never will be enough.
- God knows you are more than enough. You are it. You are the chosen one.
- You can bring value even to richest of the rich. It is a win-win.

Q2: How can I really detach from a horrible past? If I keep attached to it, will it be more difficult for my business to evolve?

- You must clean and complete your past, find the emotional roots that are holding you back.
- Your incomplete past will affect your present.
- Look at your past and say, "I am grateful I lived through this, because of this I can add more value to the world. I can add awareness to the world. I am not saying what happened to me was okay, I am recognizing it was part of my own evolution to transform people's lives."

Tiffany

Q1: What's the best way to separate your personal and professional brand? How can they be intertwined yet have separate identities?

- Look at the examples of Richard Branson, Oprah, and similar individuals. They are their brand. When living your life's *purpose* there is no such separation.
- You only want to separate your business and personal life when you are not really living your *purpose.*
- When living your *purpose,* you can have it all. There is time for everything.

Q2: How does service and being in congruence with my *purpose* equate to success?

- The way you are living in congruence with your values behind the scenes will be reflected in your income.
- How you are on the inside reflects on the outside.
- How you show up in the world, especially with people who don't need you, will be manifested in the results of your business.

Q3: How does one stay present when there are circumstantial distractions?

- The best way to be present is to acknowledge what's going on in your life.
- Make time to honor your emotions, be in your Ego if you need to, and then shake it off.
- Choose to surround yourself and share with those who can lift you up and stand for your greatness.

CHAPTER 8

Spiritual Orgasm

I have your attention, right? I expect that some of you reading this book may have jumped forward to this chapter just to know what on earth this crazy woman is talking about…I see you!

Orgasm is known as the peak of sexual excitement. This wonderful experience is a powerful feeling of physical sensations and pleasure which includes a discharge and release of accumulated erotic tension.

People of all ages can have orgasms. I still remember the first time I experienced one. I was still a little girl and without any sexual knowledge. Although I was still too young to know what sex and orgasms were all about, I still recall loving the strong sensation and wonderful feeling that sent tingles throughout my body. I was asleep, and my powerful orgasm awakened me.

Naturally, I was inquisitive about learning and understanding what was happening to my body. I am fortunate that my mom gave me a book to read so I could learn all about the changes that were occurring to me. It is called *The What's Happening to My Body? Book for Girls: A Growing-up Guide for Parents and Daughters* by Lynda Madaras.

This extraordinary book opened a wonderful world of knowledge and provided me with a better understanding of my body. This book and my mother helped me become aware of all my body's functions and I developed a healthy relationship with my sexuality. I was blessed that through my personal experiences growing up, I never saw my body or sexuality as something bad or dirty. Throughout my *purpose*-filled journey I have encountered many people who think the total opposite. Some of them previously found their relationship with sex, sexuality, and lack of orgasms to be challenging.

Being in Essence honors our body. As we evolve and grow, we learn to honor our sacred sexual energy. Our Essence's sexual energy is a powerful source of creativity for our *purpose*. This energy can be nurtured with or without a partner, yet we can only flourish when who we really are, Essence, has a connection.

The Ego wants to disconnect us from every form of our Essence, including our sacred sexual energy. It uses this powerful tool to manipulate and keep people trapped in circles of destruction and suffering.

ESSENCE REMINDER

Our sexual energy will contribute to our evolution, health, and consciousness when being in Essence. From Ego, it will distract us and lead to darkness.

Intimacy and sex are two different things. There are couples who may have never been intimate but have had sex. To be intimate is to be naked in our souls. It requires people in Essence ready to honor God in their connection. It means being fully present to the gift of the moment. Intimacy equals love; first self-love and then loving the other person. We can only give what we possess.

In his book, *Think and Grow Rich*, Napoleon Hill says:

> *When driven by this desire, men develop keenness of imagination, courage, willpower, persistence, and creative ability unknown to them at other times. So strong and impelling is the desire for sexual contact that men freely run the risk of life and reputation to indulge it. When harnessed, and redirected along other lines, this motivating force maintains all its attributes of keenness of imagination, courage, etc., which may be used as powerful creative forces in literature, art, or in any other profession or calling, including, of course, the accumulation of riches.*

When we share our sexual energy, we share our entire self. When we receive sexual energy from another person, we're not only receiving their Essence, but the impact of their Ego. This is why sex is so powerful. The energetic residual trace of ourselves is found in every one of our lovers, so we must be present with what we are receiving.

Homeplay:

Cleaning your sexual energy

No matter how many people you have been with, there is a way to clean and purify your sexual energy.

- Why do you want to clean your sexual energy?
- Make sure you have the manifestation of self-love and living your *purpose* as a key component of your reason *why*.
- Taking responsibility for everything you experience in your sexual energy will liberate you from the chains of the past.
- Find the root of negative connections with your sexual energy.
- Complete with the people of your past.
- Embrace your sexual energy as part of your God-given gifts.
- Transform your relationship with your sexuality from one of Ego, attachment, and weakness to one of empowering and transformation.
- Unveil the taboos you have around sex.
- Discover your body as your temple, not just your physical vehicle.

PURPOSE

- Listen to your body, connect with your feelings and the language that it speaks.
- You know your Essence, you know your body and your sexual energy.

ESSENCE REMINDER

The suffering around our sexual energy comes from unresolved experiences of our past. It is not what happened to us but the meaning we gave it that will shape the direction of our energy.

Homeplay:

Finding the root of your emotional disconnection with your sexual energy:

Perhaps, you have emotional or physical results that are not in alignment with who you are becoming. Either you are attracting partners that cheat on you or you are cheating on them, maybe you can't connect with someone on a deep level, or choose to be alone not from a healthy and empowering standpoint, but from fear of getting hurt.

Carol, a beautiful thirty-five-year old, came to my seminar looking great on the outside. Her clothes, makeup, hair, nails, big smile, and even her job were all on point. She is what one would call picture-perfect. Yet when I looked into her eyes, all I could see was her pain. While no one in her life knew that she was going through depression and facing suicidal thoughts, I felt it. My Essence has a way of showing me what people need from me.

Her story of disconnection started when she was brutally raped when she was still a little girl. As an adult, she found herself in a relationship with abusive man who cheated on her. In one of her unconscious relationships, she wound up pregnant by a married man. She didn't know he was married until she found out she was expecting twins and shared the news with him. Feeling lost and alone, she decided to end the pregnancy.

For many years after, she carried the guilt of terminating her pregnancy. Although she tried to move forward and had many other relationships, none of them worked. She was desperate, suffering, and she wanted to end her pain at any cost.

Through our work together, she recognized that her own Ego was dragging her down and she didn't have a *purpose.* All her attention was on her "problem." She stopped seeing all the wonderful things she had to live for in her life.

Her Ego embraced the fact that she had been a victim for more than thirty years. The Ego doesn't care what it costs you or your Essence, its goal is to win and ensure that its target remains a victim. Carol realized that her Ego was winning a destructive game it had created of her life. She thought she didn't have a choice in the matter, but she did and decided to do something about it.

She recognized she was not the voice in her head screaming that she was a whore, a bitch, a bad woman. She learned to listen to the voice of her Essence. During her sessions with me, she participated in my root coaching. This process had her go back in time in her mind to discover her emotional root of when she was sexually abused. She explored and felt the feelings of terror, confusion, and the guilt. She listened to the declaration of the Ego that said to her, "You are dirty, you will never be enough."

Through coaching, she was able to acknowledge the impact of the lie the Ego was telling her. Her Ego was choosing her partners and damaging her relationship with her beautiful self. She was blinded and could not see her light.

Her false beliefs were challenges to her willingness and ability to trust. She was selecting abusive partners so her Ego could be right. She stayed in damaging relationships so her Ego could keep her in a victim status. It was costing her happiness—the price was everything.

In the process of healing, she went back to the painful moment one more time with the eyes of her Essence. This was her first experience observing herself and feeling God's presence, listening to God's voice, and realizing she was never alone.

She was in tears, shaking, and could hear God saying, "I am here, you are not alone. I am with you. You are love, you are pure, you are loved." This was contradictory to what the Ego said, and this is because the Ego was fighting to keep her in victim status.

Carol was ready to heal, and she could hear God's message clearly and feel His presence. Sometimes it is in our most difficult moments we can truly see how much God loves us. She understood that God's love kept her alive because he had a bigger *purpose* and mission for her.

Carol surrendered and completely let go. She chose to no longer carry the weight of her experience. Of course, this was not okay for her Ego because the power to continue defying her was gone.

She took responsibility not for the actions of her abuser, but for allowing this to damage her life. She chose the true God within her. For first time in her life, she truly felt free. She found her *purpose* of being a transformational coach and, within, her mission to help survivors of sexual abuse. She wrote a letter to her twins and found peace and closure.

If you had an abortion and you feel guilty, please let go of your guilt. All you need to do is take responsibility for your actions and send love to the souls who are not here physically, but will always be connected with you in Essence love.

Even if you don't agree that life starts at conception, be complete with the time this form of life was within you. These angels make karmic agreements with you before you are even born to help you evolve, that is all. From now on, you have a choice without judgment. It is your body, your life, you choose.

In my case, I chose life. Yet I absolutely respect what women choose to do with their bodies. As you evolve, the ending of life becomes unnecessary as you will no longer manifest this type of gift. You will receive gifts in other forms. Yes, you read it correctly. I am both pro-life (my personal choice) and pro-choice. I believe that all women should have the ability to decide what to do with their bodies.

This may be controversial for the Egos that are trying hard to dislike me or this book. It's okay, because I stopped trying to please everybody a long time ago. Women, be free. Educate yourselves and protect your rights, your choice. In the end, follow your Essence in every step you take.

Carol transformed the most awful experience of her life into a story of inspiration for thousands of people. She became a prominent life coach and philanthropist. She is now happily married to her soulmate and is expecting a daughter. She confirms that she has experienced multiple orgasms in both physical and spiritual forms, and one is in her own new relationship with God.

It is important that you know you can always start again, no matter what has happened in your past. Your experiences don't have to define you if you listen to God's plan for your life. Each person in your life has been a teacher to share with you in a different manner that will help you choose your best way. This teacher will help you recognize your greatness even if it contrasts the opposite approach.

A VALENTINE'S MESSAGE: LOVE YOURSELF FIRST. TODAY AND EVERY DAY

St. Valentine's day is a special day to celebrate love and friendship. Many people forget that throughout their life, the most important relationship is with themselves. As you heal your relationship with your divine self, you open the space to create a new plateau of inner peace.

HERE ARE FIVE KEY PRINCIPLES TO AN EXTRAORDINARY REMINDER

1. Love yourself first. We cannot give or receive what we don't have. For you to love and be loved, you must first experience love and respect for yourself. Many people are searching outside of themselves to find what's missing

within. They end up in an ongoing cycle of emptiness and unfulfillment. Recognize that you must be your priority always. Your self-love will bring out your best and will move you to be and give your best.

2. Be happy with or without someone. No one can make you happy. Happiness is a choice you must make every day, no matter your present circumstances or the people around you. When you put your happiness in the hands of someone else, you are not taking responsibility for your life. By giving this power away, you become a *victim.* You are a perfect and whole human being God created to exist and share happiness with others. When you are happy, you attract happy people and happy relationships. Don't wait to honor your joy. Be happy *now*!

3. Let your *purpose* be the center of your life. Without a *purpose,* nothing works. For you to find meaning and fulfillment, you must find and live your life's *purpose.* Why are you here? What is your passion? What is your mission? *Purpose* will empower you to honor your legacy. When you are living your *purpose,* and focusing your attention on contribution, there is no time for drama. You will be too busy serving others. Your relationship with your loved ones will support and add to your *purpose*-driven life.

4. Be clear about your values. Have clarity about your top values and make sure you honor them. Be clear what is and is not negotiable in your life. For your beloved or

potential "significant other" to respect and honor your values, you, my dear one, must make certain you are acknowledging their values, loving them, and respecting them fully.

5. Learn and grow. Let go of your past and learn from it. Understand that everything that has happened to you in your life, including painful experiences, have been part of a perfect plan for your evolution. These experiences will continue to manifest in many forms until you "get" the lesson. A healthy relationship can only grow in a clean space. Take care of cleaning your space first so you will then have the space for the magical relationship God has in store for you.

FINDING THE ROOT OF NEGATIVE CONNECTIONS WITH YOUR SEXUAL ENERGY

1. Meditate or pray to ask your Essence for guidance.
2. Identify the specific results you would like to transform.
3. What is *sexual* energy for your Ego?
4. What is *sexual* energy for your Essence?
5. Which one do you choose?
6. What actions in your relationship separate you from your pure *sexual* energy today?

7. Take responsibility for your results.

8. Clean the space with yourself. Write a letter forgiving yourself and every partner in your life.

9. Burn or bury your letter.

10. Listen to mantras of healing and let the vibration of the mantras enter your heart.

11. Write your transformed vision about yourself in your relationships.

12. Write the actions you will take. For example: Stay single and date yourself, be open to manifest your twin flame, be open to dating and exploring. There is no right or wrong answer. Let your Essence choose the right way for you.

13. Don't try to stop your fears, they will never go away. The only thing you can do is stop identifying with the fears and be in Essence. Act in spite of them.

14. Identify how it feels in Essence to know you are divine. Write it down.

15. Make a list of all the things you are grateful for from your past relationships/lovers/experiences.

Spiritual orgasms occur when you are no longer a slave of your Ego. It can happen during meditation, just by the pure vibration of your sacred energy. It can also happen on a physical level when you are intimately connected to yourself or the person you love. Once you experience a spiritual orgasm, you will feel a profound sense of oneness.

HEALING YOUR INNER CHILD

Many disconnections from our Essence come from the disconnection from our inner child. The inner child is the beginner version of ourselves, our innocence in pure form. In my retreat, The Magic of Manifestation, I facilitate deep, transformational exercises to close open circles with our inner child.

- We encourage and invite participants to bring a photo from when they were children, preferably age seven and under. If they don't have a picture, they draw a picture of themselves, or find a picture of a child that looks like themselves. We ask them to see their inner child with the eyes of their heart.

- As you read this, I invite you to do the same.

    - Get a recent photo of yourself.

    - Sit down with your picture of yourself as a child and have a conversation with him/her.

    - As you talk to your inner child, take this opportunity to clean up the space there. This will give you access to a life of freedom and power.

Ask yourself for forgiveness for the time he/she was alone and for any time they felt unprotected.

- Remind yourself you were never alone, and that God was with you all the time. Talk to yourself and tell yourself you love yourself with all your heart. Tell your inner child how much you love and admire yourself, and how important they are to you.

Read this to them:

My beautiful child of God, you are perfect just the way you are. You are light, you are love, and loved by me and God. I embrace every part of you and I honor every part of you. You taught me to be free, and as I got older, I forgot. I am sorry I hurt you, and I am sorry I forgot about you for a time in my life. Please know that I was lost. I didn't find myself, but I found you.

For so long, I ran away from your innocence, and from you. I forgot that it is from your vulnerability that I can do great things. I ask for your forgiveness. I forgive myself. I vow to you that I will love you unconditionally. I will nurture your light with my dance. I will nurture your strength with my songs.

I vow I will play once again. I vow to let you be yourself and to create with you. I vow to run with you, to stop and hug a tree with you, and to kiss a flower with you. I vow to touch a beautiful animal and feel his heart. I vow to look at the sky and see your eyes in the moon.

I promise to talk to the stars and listen to the messages they have for us. I promise in your name to live my purpose every day, for it is with your power that we will create amazing things together. I ask you to trust me as I now trust you back. I vow to surround us with loving people. I vow to learn each and every day. I ask you to believe as I believe in us again. We will always be together for life in these and many lives more. I love you.

Now take your recent photo.

What do you see? What is missing? What do you say to her/him? Is there anything to complete? Is there anything you need to ask forgiveness for? This is your time to be free. Take this time to clean, to let go, and heal. Do not waste another day without the delicious taste of joy!

What beautiful things can you celebrate about yourself? Say them out loud, embrace yourself, and love yourself. You earned it, you are here.

Read this to the newest version of yourself looking at your photo:

Gorgeous creature, here you are. You have nothing to stop you from becoming the woman/man you are destined to become. You are a warrior, a leader, a beautiful manifestation of God.

I want to thank you for everything you do, even for the little things that many times I don't appreciate about you. Let me tell you how amazing you are, even though sometimes you don't believe it. You know our Ego does not like to let us talk.

I honor your courage to grow, and I acknowledge you for all you give, for all the invisible acts of kindness, for the extra time, the hugs, for being there for those who need you the most. I honor you for not losing faith even after you fall.

SHARE IT

I acknowledge you for not giving up on helping others even when they were not there for you. I honor you for remaining standing tall and your willingness to start again. To dare to follow your dreams and manifest what you really deserve. I honor you for having balls/ovaries strong enough to stand up for yourself. I honor all the times you took a stand for yourself and said no. I celebrate the times you dance alone, walk alone, laugh alone, pray, and recognize that in the end you were never alone. As we heal together, we will rise together. As we let go of our past, we let our inner child shine through. Listen to them talk and let's be happy! Let's allow our light to shine so brightly that only the sun will be able to match it.

We are ready to share our purpose with the world, to share our gift, and we are ready to receive what God has in store for us. You are a star, my love, you are it, you have it all. I loved you, I love you, and I will always love you.

Now put the two photos together.

Listen to the advice of that inner child for you. Let them connect to you, feel, and express himself/herself fully. Get used to the feeling of having the two of you together.

ESSENCE REMINDER

"Love is the bridge between you and everything."

—Rumi (My favorite poet)

THE POWER OF ACKNOWLEDGEMENT

When you edify someone you love, care about, admire, or are grateful for, the entire Universe responds.

Authentic acknowledgement is food for the Essence. Many people will wait until a person is no longer with them to talk about them. Don't wait until someone's transition to express your heart's feelings. You don't know when this person will leave their physical form.

Edify those you love today. Call them and meet them in person.

Express your gratitude and what they mean to you. Some of them will be surprised or even worried, possibly thinking that something bad is going on. People are just not used to receiving special edification.

When honoring someone you love, do it one-on-one. Take these steps in front of people you both know, and if possible in public settings. Acknowledgment has transformational power, as the person will become more of what you edify.

Homeplay:

1. Create a list of people you would like to acknowledge and why you want to do so.
2. Make sure to include things you admire about each person and list highlights in your relationship.
3. Schedule the time to edify them on your calendar.
4. Honor your word and play full out.

5. Overdeliver in your acknowledgement.
6. Essence bonuses: give them a handwritten card, meaningful gift, and spend quality time together.

WHAT DOES BEING *IN LOVE* MEAN?

Being "in love" is love within. This type of love comes from your heart. Everything we have comes from our *purpose*. The acceptance of unconditional love is to embrace all of who I am, my *purpose*, and my love for the world. This means I can be in love with others and my relationship with God.

I believe we *are* love, and that it is the most powerful force in the Universe. When we connect from that infinite place of love, it's possible to make a difference in this world.

ESSENCE REMINDER

"I invite you to dare to step into your greatness. Playing small is a game of the Ego. Living your greatness is being *humble."*

—Karen Hoyos

A WORD FROM ESSENCE

Before meeting Karen Hoyos, my marriage was on the brink of divorce. During the seminar, Karen coached me through a forgiveness exercise, which allowed me to release a burning hatred for a person I felt had severely wronged me and my family. It was one of the most profound experiences of my entire life.

I learned to stop acting from my Ego, and to start acting from my Essence. This allowed me to let go of all the anger and resentment I had been carrying. It was the first step toward joining my wife in healing our relationship. Today, we are a healed family. There are no words that can do justice to how grateful I am to Karen for that.

—Mark Dana, Entrepreneur

CELEBRATE

When living your life's *purpose,* life can become one big celebration. When we get into the habit of honoring ourselves, people around us, and our experience, we begin to understand that there are no mistakes in life, only opportunities to learn and evolve.

When something is not going the way you planned, know something amazing is about to happen. Be patient and take the time to appreciate what is present right now in your life and what is possible in your life beyond what is not working.

You can even create what is missing as long as you know there is nothing wrong with you or the world. When we make a situation wrong, we lose the opportunity to see the magic of transformation unfolding right in front of our eyes.

Celebrate life, every day. The fact that you are here breathing, that you can read, listen, touch, and taste life is a privilege. When we celebrate life, we honor and acknowledge the Universe for blessing us. As your focus expands, so will your blessings. The famous quote, "Count your blessings," is a tool to multiply them.

ESSENCE REMINDER

Celebration = Gratitude = Blessings

When my twins Estevan and David were babies, I would celebrate every milestone they had. I even have a calendar of their first year with every single change in their growth and development. What happened after that first year? When life kicks in, we get used to our magical life as being "normal" and the magic disappears. Commit to keep the fire of your Essence. When you celebrate you remember how blessed you are!

Every day can be a holiday. We don't need a specific date to honor who we are, our parents, or our friends. Celebrate any important holiday, don't be limited by those. Be open, flexible, and spontaneous and you will start feeling lighter and even younger.

LAUGH OUT LOUD (LOL)

The Ego takes life seriously, whereas the Essence loves humor. It can be silly and fun loving. Essence doesn't care what people think, for it knows those thoughts will not touch or hurt them. Science has proven that humor can heal the body.

It is important you learn to relax and let joy into your heart to maximize its health benefits. Use your LOL at least once a day Find a reason to laugh and not to be angry. When you laugh, the Universe responds with more reasons to make you have fun.

Let's do a test. Read this:

> "What did the Buddhist ask the hot dog vendor?
> 'Make me one with everything.'"

Did you laugh? All I can say is LOL!

Tips to activate your Essence fun:

- Find at least five reasons to smile every day.
- Smile at two strangers in the street.
- Give free hugs at least once per day.
- Laugh out loud at least once a day.
- Dance as if you are the lead performer in a Broadway musical.
- Walk in the rain.
- Walk with no shoes in the grass, sand, or any surface that feels good.
- Make out with a tree (LOL).
- Eat dessert first.

SHARE IT

- Kiss a little longer and give an extra kiss.
- Say, "I love you" multiple times a day.
- Have at least one orgasm daily (especially you women). Men, practice injaculation. (For those of you who may not be familiar with the technique, injaculation is the process of distinguishing the difference between male orgasm and ejaculation. It is through this process a man can have multiple orgasms during his sexual experience.)

CHAPTER 9

The Spotlight is on You!

Your process of evolution will be transformed from an unconscious evolution to a conscious one. Your reaction to the circumstances presented to you will not be as a victim of what life throws at you. You will recognize your true self (Essence) and become aware of who you are not (Ego). You are the one responsible for the reality you are creating. You will become a conscious transformational evolutionist.

Every step you take has an intention of contribution to the entire world. Your focus is on living your *purpose*, being congruent with your vision, and reflecting the impact you are standing for. One of my favorite quotes from Gandhi is, "Be the change you want to see in the world."

Being the change we want to see in the world requires a commitment that expands beyond what others can see in us. It is a commitment that moves us to always be the best version of ourselves. It's a commitment that reminds us that as humans we will do things people call "mistakes." We understand that those are just opportunities to clean up our poopoo, take responsibility, learn, grow, and share the lesson learned.

The need to have superficial conversation without an intention to make an impact is gone! This can be confronting for the Ego. As we become more aware of our *purpose*, the feeling of loneliness and watching how most people are can be unsettling for the Ego.

You may ask, "How can we contribute without separating ourselves from those who are not on the same path?" The Ego wants to be separated from the rest. It wants to fight, and it tries to convince us that we are beneath or better than other people who are not on our same path. This new experience of life creates the space for the "new age Ego." This spiritual Ego can be more dangerous than the ordinary one.

As people start expanding, learning, reading, receiving certifications, and becoming part of the personal development movement, so does the Ego. The spiritual Ego is born when we start the process of personal growth. Keep in mind that the Ego is more clever and has new tools to convince us to do what goes against the Essence and supports its actions with great arguments.

The spiritual Ego is more silent, settled, and is letting you think it may have disappeared. However, don't let your Ego fool you. It's not going anywhere. The Ego is waiting for the perfect moment to attack with new strategies. Therefore, many people on a spiritual path are so turned off, surprised, and shocked when they do things they have already overcome.

The spiritual Ego will let you believe you've got it all under control, that you already know it all, and you have arrived. Essence knows that there is no arriving in this life, as we are always evolving. We simply change destinations. Your soul is already transformed, so your higher self knows there is nothing you must do to be whole because you already are whole! I previously mentioned that we have many games to play—I view life like a game in sports. We play full-out and give our best effort on the court of life for us to win. We play in many forms and create numerous possibilities to fulfill our *purpose*. This is so we can help the world to fulfill its ultimate *purpose*: To consciously evolve all into oneness. When the norm becomes all people sharing collective awareness of one's *purpose*, peace on Earth will be possible. The soul knows this. The Ego doesn't believe it's possible.

MODUS OPERANDI OF THE SPIRITUAL EGO

The mission of the spiritual Ego is to dominate you at all costs. It already knows you can master its ordinary form, so it will use all the knowledge in your mind to also evolve in a more powerful way using spirituality as the best way to go in disguise.

Our unconscious self has many forms and uses different weapons. When it can no longer win by force, it will enter various soft types of manipulation. You cannot hate it. If you reject, fight, or ignore it in any way, it will become stronger. The ultimate *purpose* of the Ego is to separate you from everything—your true self, other people, your *purpose*, your abundance, your health—so eventually it will have all the power over you and what you do.

As I evolved in my own personal journey as a coach, I met my spiritual Ego face-to-face. Imagine Carmen (my unconscious self) with a white long rope, a third eye with fake eyelashes, a push up bra, and a lotus flower tattoo right on top of her cleavage. Hahahaha! I just made all of this up to make a point. Carmen is usually controlling, like a dominatrix (insert whip!). When I use her to open doors and to engage people, she can come back to me with spiritual reason to do what she wants. Yes, this is smart, for sure.

RAISING YOUR STANDARDS

I am aware, conscious and present, of the way I take care of my body and my health. Years ago, I made the choice to become a vegan. I choose to eat organic food at home and mostly organic when I am eating out. I exercise five times or more per week and I don't drink any alcohol, including wine. I stay away from caffeine and meditate daily. My sleep habits include getting about four hours of sleep. My body does not need much time to recover and I have been blessed that that is all that is required for me to have abundant energy to keep up with my beautiful and crazy mission.

I am also fortunate that when I go for my annual visits and check-ups, I am told my physical appearance and my organs are acting as if they are ten years younger than my age. I know some of your Egos must be saying "oh please, Miss Perfect," or "I could never do that," or "I could never give up alcohol or meat or mediate or…."

PURPOSE

On a serious note, I know it may sound too good to be true. It may sound like I am exaggerating. There was a time in my life when I thought veganism was not for me because it seemed crazy, eccentric, and not normal. I no longer think that because I truly understand what it means to be vegan. It is a lifestyle, not only a dietary choice. Let me first define what veganism is: Veganism is a way of living which seeks to exclude all forms of exploitation and cruelty to animals. These motives are for food, clothing, or any other *purpose.*

There are many ways to embrace vegan living. One thing all vegans have in common is a plant-based diet avoiding all animal foods such as meat (including fish, shellfish, and insects), dairy, eggs, and honey. This also includes many products we often may forget about, like fur, leather, or products that have been tested on animals.

The choice has been so positive for me and I know it may seem different to many folks who have not chosen to live their lives the same way. I want to give the best of me to the world and be as healthy and energetic as possible so I can to fulfill my mission. It is not because I am perfect or want to be better than other people, I simply know that by taking care of my body and choosing to do whatever it takes it will help to also end suffering to all beings, including animals.

There are great documentaries that provide specific science behind why being vegan is great for our health as well as for our environment. They also cover why veganism is critical as we consider the ethical treatment of animals.

SHARE IT

This is my list of recommended documentaries I hope you will consider watching so you are able to engage with a dialogue about veganism with your Essence: *Food, Inc.*, *Earthlings*, *What the Health*, and *Forks over Knives*. Additionally, I'd like to add that a great book on this subject is *The China Study* by Doctor T. Colin Campbell.

I learned that to give my best, I must feel my best. I started seeing and experiencing the world differently. I couldn't just go shopping and leave a mess behind just because someone would pick up after me. I started seeing people and their work differently; I began honoring them and their work even more. I would take some time to chat with the person cleaning my hotel room or helping me with my bag. I began having a humanistic experience with other humans. I stopped viewing them as workers. I awakened to the impact of my actions on other people and the planet.

Taking care of the environment is often viewed as something altruistic, however, I now see it as an instinct to protect and honor our home. If we are not collecting garbage and taking it to our bed and throwing it out before we go to sleep, why would we do that with our bigger home, Earth? I started researching holistic medicine and the natural power of our bodies to self-heal. I started reading about the side effects of what I put into my body and in my family's as well. I chose to become part of the solution and no longer part of what was damaging our planet. Of course, my Ego tried to convince me that these changes were too little compared to the many people who were doing the opposite of what would be Essence-driven behavior.

My Ego tried to tell me that this time, situation, or action does not matter. I educated myself and I found that my Essence changed me.

ESSENCE REMINDER

Every day a vegan saves: 1,100 gallons of water, twenty pounds CO_2 equivalent, three hundred square feet of forest land, forty-five pounds of grain, and one animal life.

This information changed my perspective and understanding; I now know that every action counts.

TAKING A STEP FORWARD

Once a person finds their *purpose* and the ways they can make a difference, their spiritual Ego gets stronger and more judgmental towards the people who think differently. Therefore, many of my fellow vegans have a bad reputation of being "bitchy" to others who they think don't care about our planet's animals or their health.

I don't think this is true, most people just don't know. I didn't, until I educated myself about it, and even people who have a different belief or opinion must be respected beyond our views. It is okay to disagree, it is okay to take a stand so others can learn our views. It is a matter of respect and understanding that there are many paths to the same destination and there are multiple destinations as well.

SHARE IT

We are not all going to the same destination, but as we walk we can share our *purpose* so people can have a better and happier journey, or even choose to change their course. For our Egos, this is way too boring. It wants confrontation, arguments, even fights to be right, but if we are willing to listen to other views and share ours respectfully, even our spiritual Ego won't have any power.

Living my life's *purpose* is now like oxygen for me. I need to live my *purpose* as I need to breathe. I choose to live my *purpose*—it is no longer an option. You can no longer hide. You no longer have a plan B. As you take one step forward every day, so it is your commitment to be your best version. This takes you to a place of reflection, self-observation, self-coaching, self-cleaning, and shining your light. Being seen and heard is now a responsibility.

Your spiritual Ego will fight this at all costs. It will try to convince you to stay humble and small, it will try to convince you every time you are judged and criticized by others, because it will happen. If someone is not talking behind your back, making you doubt or hate your mission, you are not doing something worth it.

Every person who is living his life *purpose* will inevitably be hurt by other Egos. Your unconscious self will want to keep you safe, protect you from controversy. It will try to keep you on the "normal" level where you can be positive but not too extreme.

I say, "No, forget about normal, ordinary, safe, cool. You are here to make a difference. You are here to shift the world, to confront the status quo, to face others with love, and at the same time with the courage of being a transformed being."

People will try to drag you to where they are. They may make fun of you for your "positive thinking crap." Oh yes, they will let you know what they don't like about you, but all of this is merely a reflection of who you are.

Be confident and bold about shining your light. When you go to an event, step in knowing you are the chosen one. You are protected by God and surrounded by angels. You make a statement just by your presence, your words, your actions.

If you are called to say something, say it. Make sure your method of communication comes from your Essence and not from the need of the Ego to be right.

POWERFUL COMMUNICATOR

For you to share your *purpose*, you must be a powerful communicator. Essence communications are a challenge for the mind because most people like to think and plan exactly what they are going to do or say prior to acting.

There are steps that allow you to have better professional and personal communication with the people in your life, especially when sharing about your *purpose*:

- If you have something to say to someone, a contribution, feedback, advice, or coaching, please ask permission first. So many times, people get offended by people throwing out unsolicited advice. Asking permission is the equivalent of knocking on your friend's door when you arrive for a visit. Even if they are expecting your visit, you don't just walk into their house.

- Before delivering an important presentation or dialogue, make sure you are fully present and not in your head. Remember the declaration: "God, you speak, think, and act through me."
- If you are having a one-to-one conversation, listen first! Let the other person express their point of view and listen with the commitment of understanding, not simply reacting.
- If others don't know you, always take time to share your story. When sharing your *purpose*, this is an essential component. Even if it is in business, your story moves people to connect with you on a "heart" level and it is easier for them to be open to the information or point you are sharing. When telling your story, include:

    1. Where you are from and a little bit about your family.
    2. Your most challenging time and how you overcame it. (No matter how beautiful your life is you can always find a challenging moment that can inspire others, either from your experience or someone you love.)
    3. How you found your *purpose* and what inspires you to live it. Tell them a little about your search for *purpose*. Inform them you are not here because you had it easy, bring them into your quest.

4. Share your point, message, and product clearly. Be succinct and to the point. Make sure to highlight how it first made a difference in your own life. Don't get off subject here, be specific. People trust people they can understand.

5. Mention testimonials of people and examples of references that back up your point. In this testimonial include the before and after narrative as well as the personal title if this will edify your message.

6. Call them into action. A lot of people miss this step. People get excited about what they are doing without asking the other person what they want from them. Be specific in what you need so when sharing your *purpose* with the right people your request is heard with clarity and power.

- Ask them if they have any questions.

- Give them space in the conversation to reply with a response of *yes* or *no*. When receiving a *yes*, thank them and move on to scheduling dates and times to follow up. Otherwise it will become an emotional moment that will be lost.

- If someone says *no* to your request, don't try to convince them into doing something they are choosing not to do. Your Ego may win in manipulating them, but this won't last and eventually will hurt them and yourself.

Thank them for listening and leave the door open for the future.

- Many times, when people meet me for first time they may not be ready for my trainings and seminars. These trainings are deep, and to fully participate requires a commitment to excellence. Even if people I meet are not ready to fully participate at that time, I still plant a seed with them and many folks tell me later that they are ready to meet their *purpose*. On occasion, some individuals have taken months or years. It's always great to meet people on their terms. I know this happens because I always leave the door open for them to enter and come through it to meet their *purpose*. Many come through and stay to fulfill their *purpose*-filled mission.

Note: It is important that you truly learn and know your elevator speech/pitch. This means learning to communicate your *purpose* and what you do in less than a minute. The first thirty seconds are the most important because, like a hippopotamus closing his ears before going into the water, most people stop listening if they are not inspired by your communication.

BIG LEAGUES

We all have heard the phrase "think big" before. I prefer to say "be big," as that is who you already are. Learn and study people who are living their *purpose* and who inspire you with their results. You don't have to reinvent the wheel, but you must create your own path towards your *purpose*-filled goals. Learn from others and be willing to try what other people haven't yet explored or done.

As I was contemplating the success of my business, I asked God what is next for me with gratitude in my heart. Of course, the mind jumps and says, "what are you looking to do?" and, "what is next?" instead of being grateful with where you are in your present situation.

The reality is that my life is a dream in every way, so it can be easy for me to say here is where I stay. In my heart I can hear God's voice clearly moving me in new directions and showing me his next move, so I am not willing to stay the same.

We are growing or dying little by little throughout our lives. I prefer to keep living in my *purpose.* Did you know that in Africa a child dies every minute? This is a strong reason for not staying still and comfortable with where I am. I am grateful, yes, but there is so much to do. What is the next step for you?

SPOTLIGHT YOUR *PURPOSE*

These days you can use social media to share your voice and be heard. Radio and television are available for anyone who has an inspiring *purpose* or idea. If you don't know anyone in media, send letters, send emails, call them, and respectfully insist on building a partnership. The Ego questions your bold choices and asks you questions to try to make you diminish who you are in your own eyes. Do not listen. Your Essence determines that you are the chosen one.

ESSENCE REMINDER

You will never know the answers to the questions you don't ask.

If you have a *purpose*, it is because you have something of value to share. Think of it this way: There are people who are dying because they haven't received your gifts. Never underestimate your ability to change a life.

When meeting people of influence, think first: How can I add value into their life? Do not target what you can get more of, focus first on what you can give. When you share value from an authentic place, leaders will want to compensate you. It's a natural reaction of people who operate from the heart. Give credit to those you have learned from. Know that the way you edify your teacher will edify you as well.

People will know you are an honest person and that you value others' contributions in your life. Ask for what you deserve. Don't be afraid to negotiate. Take a stand for your values and be willing to let go of something that is not honoring who you are and what you support. When you let go of what may be an okay opportunity, extraordinary opportunities show up.

Be present and aware of with whom you interact. If possible, surround yourself with leaders and other like-minded people. If you want to fly like an eagle, going to the school of chickens won't teach you this. Observe how people act with those whom they don't need or when they are upset. Make sure their core values match yours.

It is important to surround yourself with a group of people from whom you can enjoy learning. If you are the smartest person in your group, you will need a new group for sure. Make sure you listen, take notes, act, and acknowledge them. Edify them to other people.

Equally important is to have a group to whom you can teach what you already know. Share what has worked for you so others can learn and continue the ripple effect of your wisdom.

ESSENCE REMINDER

Teaching is the ultimate quest for those living their *purpose*. You must teach to share your gifts fully and live a legacy.

Homeplay:

A. Make a list of the five people you talk the most with every day.

B. What are they teaching you and what are you teaching them?

C. Find a mentor, a coach that will take your *purpose* to the next level.

D. Network in events where you can shine your light sharing your *purpose*.

E. Contact media outlets and offer your message/product.

F. Knock on the doors of influencers in your industry and explore collaborations. You can always find value to share with them. I guarantee you have something others need. It can be knowledge, experience, resources, or connections.

THE MAGIC OF MANIFESTATION

This is the name of my retreat in which I go deep into the waters of manifestation and show you how to take yourself out of the way, so the Universe can work through you and create what, for the mind, may be impossible.

Just over one hundred years ago airplanes didn't exist. "Flight is possible for man," was the powerful statement made by Wilbur Wright, co-inventor of the first engine airplane. Naturally, people laughed and didn't believe in that "crazy" idea. Nonetheless, Wilbur, and his brother Orville who believed in him, forged ahead with total conviction and gave people the flying power of birds.

Another example is President John F. Kennedy's extraordinary words: "We choose to go to the moon. We choose to go to the moon in this decade and do the other things, not because they are easy, but because they are hard, because that goal will serve to organize and measure the best of our energies and skills, because that challenge is one that we are willing to accept, one we are unwilling to postpone, and one which we intend to win, and the others, too."

"But how can this be possible?" people asked.

President Kennedy didn't ask "How?" he simply declared "When!"

People often forget their power to manifest, and when someone tells them what can be done, they think it is only for "the lucky ones," not for them. Others will try to achieve something but may believe it will only work in *some* areas, yet deep inside they don't think it is possible to manifest it all.

The truth is that we are *all* manifesting *all* the time. Some consciously manifest the life of their dreams; others unconsciously live by default.

When you are sharing your *purpose* with the world, the magic of manifestation becomes a dance between you and your contribution. It will be always present even when you are not thinking about it. Every day you choose your *purpose*, you are choosing to manifest, you are choosing to be the co-creator of this Universe.

The following are some key distinctions I use in my retreat:

- **Clarity:** For you to manifest anything, you must be clear of what is it you want. It is important to know you must think not only what you desire but how this vision will benefit you and others. When you send the intention of serving others through your own vision, this energy will align the Universe in your favor and you will rapidly enjoy the impact of your great intentions. Every manifestation must reflect your *purpose.* It must have an intention of edifying either you, those you love, or the world to add value to your mission.

SHARE IT

- **Make a declaration:** Be aware of everything you say because your subconscious mind is recording everything as facts. Take your Essence vision and declare it to the world. How? First, write it down, thanking the Universe for the generosity of what has already been given to you even before you physically have it. Then share it passionately with all the people in your life and everyone you meet. Every time you share from your heart, the vibration of your joy will open the door of your desire for it to be manifested.

- **Schedule your success:** Put it into the Universe with a date on it. Hold yourself accountable for your success and measure the actions you are taking toward the manifestation of your *purpose*.

- **Celebrate:** Celebrating is the art of acknowledging where you are so you can create the space of where you want to go. Honor everything you have accomplished so far, the people in your life, your health, and your gifts. A grateful heart will continue manifesting more joy in the form of results to match the frequency of your choice.

- **Be alert for the signs:** When you have a clear *purpose* and vision and when you are living in transformation, the Universe will give you signs every day of what you must or must not do. Be alert to the signs, they may come in the form of songs, conversation, lessons, dreams, or revelations. Breathe life into yourself, stay present, and you will be able to see clearly.

- **Treasure map:** Many compare the treasure map to a vision board, a place where you paste pictures of the things and experiences you are manifesting. There is power in seeing a reflection of what is in your heart every day. It works as a reminder of your Essence that the best is yet to come.
    - When choosing your pictures, ask:
    - God, what do You have for me?
    - What is Your vision for me?
    - What is Your manifestation for me?

  Let your Essence guide you, because your soul knows how to direct you to choose the images that will match your vibration. Include images of the four essential areas: spirituality, relationships, health, and finances. Write a check with the amount that you are manifesting and sign it "God." Place your vision board next to your bed or on the ceiling, where you can see it every day. When you see this board, close your eyes and visualize, relish the powerful feeling of having what's already yours. When God puts a vision in your heart it is not only possible, it is a universal command.

DIVINE GUIDANCE

I invite you to imagine you are in the living room of your dream house. Your guests are the five people whom you most admire and are not yet part of your everyday circle. These people may be alive or no longer be in physical form with us. Ask them all the questions you have in your mind. While asking questions trust in the process, as God will speak through every one of them. What you need will be revealed to you.

My five people are: Jesus, Buddha, Mother Teresa, Gandhi, and Martin Luther King, Jr. We have the power to connect with their Essence at any time. This is because the Essence in them is eternal and so are their teachings. When you are living your life's *purpose*, you are treated differently by the Universe and it will reveal gifts to you that may be invisible for others.

ESSENCE DECLARATION

I am ready to accept the responsibility of my power. As I walk this path, I welcome the uncertainty of not knowing. I no longer hide my light, I give my Essence permission to shine through everything I do. I trust the process even when I can't understand the present results.

I walk by faith not by sight, I recognize the signs, I stay still to be aware, and I act when it is the right time. I don't question my Essence as I know it is clear. I recognize my Ego and its reasons. I look for the light even when it is dark. I give myself permission to believe in my powers, for God, You are the one leading my path. I am no longer afraid to fail, because failure does not exist. I learn and continue sharing the lessons that have learned in my *purpose*-driven journey. I choose to be my authentic self even if this causes confrontation with some people. I let go of the need to please others and let those who add value in my life arrive and stay with me. I cultivate meaningful relationships. I trust

PURPOSE

You, God, I trust myself, and I trust the people my Essence will attract.

I am alert and awake, even when I sleep, for everything I do is to be great. I discover hidden treasures and I receive innovative ideas to put them into action. When I need to, I ask for support and I relax and stay present with those I love. I let go of guilt when receiving compensation for my Essence work. I will never stop shining and I will teach others to let light come through their Essence. I am happy with who I am and ready to discover more manifestation of my light. I honor where I am, and I move forward to receive what is next for me. I let go of control and welcome the miracles. I am my *purpose*.

Thank you, God.

Namaste.

PART IV

HONOR IT

The last stage of *purpose* is honor. While this is no longer about you, it requires you to be fully manifested. As you start mastering the art of self-awareness, you clearly recognize when you are being your authentic self and when you are not. Lifelong commitment to your *purpose* does not depend on outside circumstances.

As you practice being in Essence and present from your transformation, you become the master of your powers. As you surrender to your destiny of greatness, new possibilities will open for you. The Universe responds more quickly to your requests and you experience being seen and protected.

Being a star in your mission is part of who you are for the world. You are no longer trying to be anything you are not. With this new state of clarity, access to what once was a dream becomes part of the reality of your Essence.

To honor your *purpose* is to honor the ultimate quest you embark on to fulfill your calling. It is to look back and see that everything was a conspiracy for you to win. God was with you all along and you were never alone. It is to live in gratitude, not because you must, but because it is your natural state. Every single encounter with your new standards is the discovery of the new abilities that were given to you with the intention of your evolution to serve humanity.

Now comes the daily practice that is required with all this powerful new space. You now need to know how to apply all this knowledge. The final part of this book will focus on the application of your knowledge and provide you with a roadmap to see how all your dreams, efforts, and actions will come together in tangible results.

CHAPTER 10

Marrying Your Purpose

The best way to know how to live, share, and honor your *purpose* is to first know where you are. I love to use the analogy of a marriage. Now, before some of you who don't believe in the institution of marriage start rolling your eyes at me, read (yes, read, not hear) me out.

The marriage I am talking about is a representation of a lifetime commitment that can't be broken by any man, woman, or child. You may think about the question of divorce and the challenges surrounding that type of separation. What I am presenting to you here is different. In this type of *purpose* marriage, divorce does not exist as an option. In this case, you no longer choose your *purpose* because your *purpose* has already chosen you. In case you haven't noticed, I am wearing a wedding dress on my cover. It was my subconscious message for you—an invitation to love; an eternal love affair.

PURPOSE

Let's start with the clarity that you want to live your *purpose* forever. If you don't, please stop reading right now because this part is not for you. If you have crystal-clear knowledge in your heart that this is it for you and you are ready to give your life for your *purpose,* then you are in the right spot! This marriage is for you.

Now some people may be crazy enough to marry their soulmate right away. *When you know, you know,* these people frequently say. I was one of those crazy ones. Once I found my *purpose,* I knew this was it, and I married it right away. I must say that I am still enjoying my honeymoon after fifteen years of marriage in 2018. For me, coaching, speaking, and transforming people's lives through every way possible is definitely my passion and it will be what I will do and who I will be for the rest of my life.

Living a life where there is not even the slight chance of being unfaithful to my *purpose* creates a sacred space. It is a safety net that nothing and nowhere else on Earth can provide to me. I walk with a sense of knowledge, a sense of fulfillment, and a sense of belonging. Before living my *purpose*, I never had the same sense of fulfillment.

It has become my lifetime mission to help people to live *purpose*-filled lives. This is the reason why this book has come to fruition and has been birthed after a pregnancy of fifteen years shaping the Essence of this content. Yes, I married my *purpose* while pregnant with this book. Go ahead and judge me if suits your pleasure. (Blink).

STAGES

Dating

Some people need to date around before meeting "the one." In this case, there is the group of people who have worked on other things before finding their *purpose*. If they reflect on this, they can now recognize that their true calling was present even before they fully recognized it.

It was there, all alone, until it was pointed out and accepted. Dating to find your *purpose* is completely normal. During this stage you will encounter wonderful opportunities that may be similar to your true love. This is okay. Everything you study, every job you have had, was part of this dating process to value your *purpose* when you finally identified and started living it.

In some cases, the person can find his or her *purpose* and continue to casually date because they do not feel ready and prepared to commit. However, once you find it, you cannot hide. It is like a hairy spider on your face. Hairy and smelly too, so it is fairy impossible to pretend it is not sitting there. I am not sure how I went from dating to a smelly spider, but you get the point.

If you are in this stage you know what you are up to doing at this point, and through reading this book you know and have identified your *purpose*.

ESSENCE REMINDER

Outer *Purpose*:

Evolution, to change.

Inner *Purpose*:

Contribution is defined by your ability to share your gifts with the world through the vehicle of your passion.

What would you do if you had all the money and time in the world to help others?

If you are choosing to date but you know you want to marry your *purpose*, don't spend more time giving away your energy to something you know will not last. Put a timeline and a deadline to your dating situation. Give a specific date to commit to exclusivity. It should be no more than three months. If, after ninety days, you are still wandering around, you are not ready.

Homeplay:

Schedule a time right now on your calendar when you will become exclusive. This does not mean you have to quit the job that you don't like, at least not yet. It means that on that date, you will start planning the quest to marry your soul mission.

Exclusivity

At this stage you declare your love to and for your *purpose*, you are committing to cultivate your relationship with it. Start training to manifest your *purpose*, reading books and materials that will teach you and give you references of other people who have fulfilled what you have chosen to do on your path and how you plan to get there.

You may have decided you are fine with sharing your time with and working for a job that has nothing to do with your *purpose*. Maybe you truly like it. For those of you who simply hate it, just know that at this point it is just a matter of time. In this stage, you start the cleaning of your space to become congruent with your mission. You talk to people about your new relationship, you inspire others, and let others inspire you. You make a declaration for what is to come in your life. You know what is going to happen no matter what. You may not know the *how*, but you are now clear of your *purpose*.

This stage of action comes with a date, an important date when you will propose to your Essence and get engaged to your *purpose* once and for all.

Homeplay:

Schedule on your calendar now the time when you will become engaged. This means you will enter an era where you will plan to completely fulfill your calling. You will plan your transition from where you are to where you want to be in your *purpose* and mission.

Engagement

Time for the ring. Yes, I know, I am a romantic to my core. In this stage, you know the marriage is happening and you are celebrating it. You dedicate most of your time to do whatever it takes to cultivate your relationship with your *purpose*. If you are still in a job that has nothing to do with your *purpose*, start the transition and the plan of how your life will be when you are fully living your *purpose*. In this stage, it is important to receive guidance—coaching on how to learn to make a living with your *purpose*. This is part of what I teach in my training: how to create a successful business to generate financial abundance exclusively with your *purpose*. This is the time to fully clear your spiritual relationship with money as I guided you in how to do in chapter six. I invite you to revisit this chapter as it has excellent business tools for your transformational business. In this stage, you are investing in yourself and in your business. You talk and learn from people who have successful, long, and healthy marriages with their *purpose*. In this stage, you may also start working with someone who is going to prepare you for when you are independent. In this stage, you volunteer your time with organizations or companies that are part of the industry of your *purpose* with the intention of learning the ins and outs of your industry. This is an essential time to network and meet new connections that take you a step closer to the manifestation of your *purpose*. Here you are selective about who you share your time with, you are aware about your conversations, for you know your time is becoming your most valuable treasure. You learn, read, and write every day something about your calling. Start practicing your *purpose*. It's like touching the water while getting ready to swim.

You must choose a date for the big day. Depending on the person, it can be anything from six months to a year. It can be less, but definitely no more than that. I have found that if someone is really ready to fulfill their *purpose*, their Ego will never be. The circumstances won't be perfect, but they will be in alignment if this is what you choose.

Homeplay:

It's time to schedule your wedding date! This date is extra special. This can be a day, a week, or a whole month. When scheduling your wedding, consider the following aspects: During this time, you will finally marry your *purpose*. You will no longer share your time with anything that distracts from your *purpose*. You quit your non-*purpose* job or any other activity that interferes with your sole *purpose*. There are no more part-times here. Your attention, intention, energy, and action are fully directed to the manifestation of your *purpose*. Pick this date wisely, for there won't be any going back.

Marriage

The dream is no longer a dream, the vision is no longer a vision, your future is now your present, and your *purpose* is who you are. This is an exclusive marriage. You vow to fulfill your *purpose* until you take your last breath. You vow to give all of your heart, your attention, your energy, and your love to it. You vow to honor your *purpose* even in moments of difficulty because you know challenging times will come. You promised to nurture your relationship by learning, continuing to grow, and creating a support system around you.

When facing distraction, you will say no, and when given opportunities you will filter them always with your *purpose* in mind. In moments of doubt, you will remember it is not you doubting, it is your Ego. You will listen to your Essence and do everything to go back to consciousness. You promise to be the best version of yourself and to take care of your mind, body, and spirit. Your life will become a reflection of your *purpose*. You will protect the quality of what enters your mental and heart space.

You will learn how to help other people walk into their ultimate quest. Seeking guidance from mentors, high profile alliances, and friends will be the norm. You will be the leader of your life, *purpose,* and legacy. Your light will illuminate those around you wherever you go. You will be too big to hide. There won't be any more trying in your life—either you do or you don't. You will honor your *yes* and be congruent in saying your *no*. You will reflect on every one of your choices and make changes as you grow, even if they seem radical to most people.

Mediocrity won't be sharing space with you anymore. You will be quick to jump into action. Taking responsibility for your actions and cleaning your space will be like breathing for you. Every chance you have, you will mention and share your *purpose,* and every person you encounter will either teach you something or be the recipient of your gift.

Homeplay:

With this Homeplay it's time to go big or stay home. Make a big public announcement of your marriage, register your business, celebrate with those you love. Hold an event where you present your mission to your circle and to a potential contributor to your *purpose*. Be ready to receive skepticism from some and praise from others. Don't let anything negative detract from your celebration. Answer questions and give people specific ways they can help you to raise funds, mention the nonprofit organization that your *purpose* will be supporting, and inspire everyone with your light and love for humanity. Change the way people see you, as who you are has been transformed.

After the Honeymoon Stage

It is not possible to talk about *purpose* and not talk about what happens after you are finally married. You will have ongoing magical moments and multiple spiritual orgasms. In some cases, you will encounter difficult times, especially in finance. Even after healing your relationship with money this area is usually a thermometer for your faith and commitment. Be prepared for drastic changes, for unexpected news. Stay present and focus on your *purpose*, knowing your problems will pass. After every storm there is a calm. Please be patient. Don't let the Ego take over because it will use every tool in the book to sabotage your spiritual marriage.

When facing difficulties, invest your time and energy into talking and learning from people who were previously in the same position as you. They will know what to share to keep you on track. Watch inspirational movies based on true stories. I love watching films about how various situations became the anchor for success.

Some of these movies are: *The Pursuit of Happyness, What the Bleep Do We Know?, A Beautiful Mind, Life of Pi, The Blind Side, Coach Carter, Gandhi, The Peaceful Warrior, Finding Nemo, Coco,* and many more. Mediate, pray, dance, and laugh as much as you can.

ESSENCE REMINDER

The darkest hour of all is the hour before dawn.

A CONVERSATION ABOUT PARENTING AND CONNECTING WITH THE FUTURE

Because I used the metaphor of marriage, I can't help but think of all of you who constantly ask me questions about parenting. Maybe you are a parent, or want to be, or you just want to contribute to a kid you love, or help a parent who is close to your heart.

The truth is that I believe that our babies, kids, and teens are definitely our future and are the ones who will carry on the legacy of *purpose*.

I am sharing with you the principles I apply in the beautiful process of being a mother and that have helped thousands as well. There is no guide for parents; your own Essence will know what do. These principles will serve as pointers to your own wisdom. I include this part here because if we help our kids heal, evolve, and succeed in the manifestation of their *purpose*, they won't have to struggle to find their way. They still must go through their own challenges, but the experience and the quality of their life will definitely be much different.

Conception and Pregnancy

Regardless if your baby is a surprise or planned, it is already within you, so welcoming your baby form the moment you know of his/her existence will make a big difference for them. They can feel the energy of acceptance, love, or rejection. Stay calm and fully present.

As a fetus grows, it's constantly getting messages from its mother. It's not just hearing her heartbeat and whatever music she might play to her belly, it also gets chemical signals through the placenta. A study which will be published in *Psychological Science*, a journal of the Association for Psychological Science, finds that this includes signals about the mother's mental and emotional state.

If the mother is depressed, that affects how the baby develops after it's born. Read to your baby. If both parents are present, sing, talk to the baby as if it is already born. Play classical music and mantras directly to the belly. This will help your baby learn how to be calm. Let them know how much you love them, that you are ready for them, and that you promise to be the best version of yourself for them. Enjoy the ride even when it does not feel good. You will inevitably feel pain. Embrace it instead of rejecting it. As you embrace the challenges with love you will feel the presence of love.

Baby–Twelve Years Young

These are key years in the subconscious programming in your child. Play meditation music for them and mantras as well.

Pray with them, talk to them in complete sentences, and know they have the capacity to absorb everything you're saying. Enjoy each stage, for they do grow very fast. People used to say that about my twins and I was like, yeah, and now they are the ones carrying me around.

Teach them by actions, for they speak louder than words. When you are with them be fully present, get off your phone or other distractions. When working, let go of guilt for not being with them and, when you are with them, enjoy your time. Put in your calendar important dates like celebrations and school trips and events.

If you put your kids first in your schedule you won't find yourself trying to squeeze them in. Talk to their teachers and learn about their process and, at the same time, don't be attached to their grades. Albert Einstein was not a genius in school. Grades don't measure your kid's intelligence, they are only a requirement of the school system. If possible, choose a school that focuses on the strengths of your child instead of their own cookie-cutter agenda.

I enrolled my kids in a progressive school in New York. They would meditate every day, repeat mantras, and do declarations. I am clear that not every person has access to this type of education, but you can complement it well at home. Be present about what they watch at home, everything is teaching them something. Avoid violence in what they watch, and if there is any, take time to explain to them what they are watching.

Acknowledge your child's successes and great results constantly and talk with your child about what does not work.

Don't hit or scream at your child, it will only create more violence and the idea that this is the way. Create agreements rather than rules. Talk to them when they do something that is not in alignment with your agreements.

Keep your promises to them and clean up with them when you don't. Teach them to say no. Teach them sexual education when they are young so they don't have to learn about it from their friends, as this conversation most likely will come as they grow.

Introduce them to art, sports, science, math, and spiritual practices with different vehicles than the ones in school. Trust them, believe them even if sometimes they don't keep their word. They will learn forgiveness and compassion from you, as well as being conscious about their health, the impact they have on the planet, the vulnerability of animals, and how they can make a difference in the world.

And of course, introduce Ego and Essence so if they have a tantrum they know it is not them, it's their little guy in their head. A great book recommendation is *Milton's Secret* by Eckhart Tolle. Most important of all, show them your love in every form. As they grow they will learn to express it too.

Teens

People often say things like, *Oh, it must be difficult to have twin teen boys, oh my*! I quickly reply, *No!* Some look at me with disbelief, trying to understand my answer. I always say being a parent has been a beautiful blessing because this is how I see it. Start by getting rid of those beliefs that limit your connection with your teen.

They are simply humans trying to find their way. Focus on all the great things they do. As you celebrate them, they will do them more. Give them access to technology but do not let it run their lives. My kids didn't have cell phones until they were fourteen. I focused on giving them books so they could cultivate their love for reading and exercising their brain.

Sit with them, invest quality time with them. Eat together without distractions. Be open to learning from them, for they are also your teachers. Bring awareness to them about the world conflicts, politics, and religion, and teach them to accept and respect others, even what they don't agree.

Teach your children to take a stand and say something when they see injustice. Manners will always be an asset for them. Teach them to honor their elders, give back, appreciate what they have, and accept what they don't have. Teach them all the principles in this book and help them understand. Do vision boards together. Before going to sleep, ask them to mention ten things they are grateful for in their lives. Always include them in yours. Have fun with them, enjoy the process. Share your difficulties; ask them for advice. Be vulnerable with them. Teach them to manage and grow money. Understand their journey even if sometimes it is difficult. Let go of control and let presence lead your way together. Show them your love every day, in every shape and form.

A beautiful poem for you parents of teens:

Memo from a Child

by Author Unknown

Don't spoil me. I know quite well that I ought not to have all I ask for—I'm only testing you.

Don't be afraid to be firm with me. I prefer it, it makes me feel secure.

Don't let me form bad habits. I must rely on you to detect them in the early stages.

Don't make me feel smaller than I am. It only makes me behave stupidly "big."

Don't correct me in front of people if you can help it. I will take much more notice if you talk quietly to me in private.

Don't make me feel that my mistakes are sins. It upsets my sense of values.

Don't protect me from consequences. I need to learn the painful way sometimes.

Don't be upset when I say, "I hate you." Sometimes it isn't you I hate but your power to thwart me.

Don't take too much notice of my small ailments. Sometimes they get me the attention I need.

Don't nag. If you do, I shall have to protect myself by appearing deaf.

PURPOSE

Don't forget that I cannot explain myself as well as I should like. That is why I am not always accurate.

Don't put me off when I ask questions. If you do you will find that I'll stop asking and I'll seek my information elsewhere.

Don't be inconsistent. That completely confuses me and makes me lose faith in you.

Don't tell me my fears are silly. They are terribly real, and you can do much to reassure me if you try to understand.

Don't ever suggest that you are perfect or infallible. It gives me too great a shock when I discover that you are neither.

Don't ever think that it is beneath your dignity to apologize to me. An honest apology makes me surprisingly warm towards you.

Don't forget that I love experimenting. I couldn't get along without it, so please put up with it.

Don't forget how quickly I am growing up. It must be difficult for you to keep pace with me but please do try.

Don't forget that I don't thrive without lots of love and understanding, but I don't need to tell you, do I?

Please keep yourself fit and healthy. I need you.

PARENTING "TO BE" LIST

Please focus on who you are being with your kids. Help your kid to identify the name of his/her Ego.

1. Guide your kids into knowing the personality of their Ego.
2. Provide experiences and conversations that will help them clarify their *purpose.*
3. Cultivate their passions.
4. Travel as much as you can with them.
5. Expose and connect them with nature.
6. Take walks with them without phones.
7. Watch inspirational movies and afterwards, talk about what you all learned.
8. Tickle them.
9. Walk in the rain with them.
10. Play sports with them.
11. Sleep with them sometimes even if they grow.
12. Praise them in public.
13. Correct them in private.
14. Take responsibility when you know you must clean up.

15. Be impeccable with your word.

16. Cry in front of them.

17. Honor their feelings and tears.

18. Live your *purpose* so they can too.

HELPING OTHERS FIND THEIR *PURPOSE*

As you transform every aspect of your life, you begin to experience integral happiness between all areas; more than balance, it transforms into a dance. Now all makes sense, even those experiences you wanted go back and delete. You have learned to embrace yourself, love yourself, coach yourself, and observe yourself.

Now all those self-actions will be reflected into the world, for the world is connected to you and you to humanity. Every change you are making in your life is changing humanity. You matter, your life matters, your choices matter, your contribution matters, your legacy matters. You are the master of your reality and you have the power to help others become masters as well.

As you start living your own *purpose*, your focus will shift. It is in this time you are calling to help other people to find and live their own *purpose*. It is natural that people will ask you how you did it. They will want to learn from you and it will be natural on your part to help them find their way.

Here I will share with you some coaching steps that will help you with this process. If you want to go deeper and become a certified coach, we have this training available through Karen Hoyos International.

- Ground, connect, and ask God to speak through you. Let go of anything that does not allow you to be fully present. Clean your space before coaching.
- Be clear of the *intentions* of the *results* you want for the person to whom you are contributing. Clarity is power.
- Acknowledge the person for their courage in asking for support. Edify them, honor them for their investment of time and energy.
- Make sure you are both in a place without distractions.
- Let them know you *see* them, that they are *safe*. In your conversation, make sure they know there is no judgment about what they are going through. At the same time, communicate from Essence your stand to make a difference in their life.
- Ask permission to go deep, to get personal right away.
- Explain to them the difference between Ego and *Essence.*
- Explain to them the definition of *purpose* and guide them into finding or confirming what their *purpose* is. Ask them to speak from Essence and not to think about their answers.
- Don't push, be present.

- You will know when they get it.
- Make sure that whatever you teach, you live, and you are still learning. Acknowledge that when doing the coaching.
- Come from your Essence and connect to their hearts.
- Reflect with them about anything in their past that they are carrying and invite them to clean it up with themselves and the people in their life.
- Always talk "action plan" and schedule it in their calendars right away.
- Ask them about their experience with your coaching.
- Request they share their breakthrough with those in their life.
- Thank them again for being willing to grow and transform their life.

FUNDAMENTAL STEPS FOR TRANSFORMATIONAL COACHING

1. Clarify what is the result the person is ready to change.
2. Make sure the person is open and willing to go deep into their own transformation.

3. Identify the person's most difficult moment in their life and how it is connected to the results they want to change.

4. Describe a vivid picture of what they saw, heard, and felt.

5. What was the limiting decision they made?

    - A declaration statement from the Ego.

6. What was the message that God (Essence) was telling you?

    - A declaration statement and reference of strength (truth).

7. Recognize the *gift*. Can you be grateful for that experience now?

8. What actions will you take?

ESSENCE Q&A

During my seminars, both online and in person, people ask me questions and I answer as many as I can. Some coaches and facilitators have told me that they want to learn how to answer from the heart and, at the same time, be effective in the impact of the answers.

I am sharing some of my secrets that are not really secrets anymore. I don't really want to keep them secrets, I want to share it all with the world, and hope this book will be a manual for all who are ready to facilitate the process of transformation in other people's lives:

System for a Session of Q&A from Essence

1. Make sure your energetic space is clean.

2. Acknowledge the audience and God.

3. Welcome them to the (name of presentation) and length of time.

4. Briefly explain the logistics and agenda for the presentation (I will share my story, I will share the topic, I will do a Q&A session, I will promote my next program and more opportunities to work with me, then Final Q&A).

How to Deliver from Essence

1. Have someone supporting you with the questions coming in. It is ideal to have a volunteer who wants to learn from you.

2. Allow yourself to be guided to which question to choose. God will pick the question most people in the room need to have answered for themselves.

3. Feel the answer in your Essence and you will receive it from God. Channel it. You will know in your Essence exactly what this person needs.

4. Confirm the person is understanding the question.

5. Ask what is present now. Let them find their own answer within.

While Answering

1. Shift the person's view from Ego to Essence (Never answer to his or her, "I will not talk to your mind; you are smarter than me and you will win," only speak to their Essence.)

2. If they have any resistance, ask them if they are open to receive your coaching.

3. Always empower them to leave the victim mentality behind and to embrace a victorious way of being. Have them accept responsibility for their results.

4. Empower them to act, including cleaning up any poopoo.

5. Give them acknowledgement for being brave and open.

SUPER TEAM

Once you are living your *purpose*, the key component to build your empire is your team. I have learned by experience that in building your transformational team, there are key components that will influence the quality of results of your *purpose*.

Have a combination of leaders in your team who are there because they want to help as volunteers and others that are part of your business's financial growth who are being compensated.

A. Volunteers

- For me, even people who get paid must go through this process as well. Being part of a transformational team is not a favor, it is an honor. There is no better way to learn that than through serving others. I have given many hours of my time volunteering. Even though we think we are giving back, we are receiving. Invite people to volunteer with you as part of their training. Once someone learns something from you, encourage them to share their time in helping others to do the same. This will help you reach even more people, as the volunteers are helping you do it because they believe in your cause and *purpose* and not because there is an agenda. Create an intention with your team. Ask them to clarify why they are there, what moves them, what they want to give, and what they want to receive as part of their participation in the super team. Acknowledge them in public and honor their contributions. Give them special gifts and discounts on your services and products only available for them. Treat them as family because they are.

B. Performance-Based Team

- This team is focused on your business growth. They are compensated financially based on their results. All my team members are either volunteers or on a commission basis. I want to promote leaders to be independent. If they are working for a salary, they may not see their full potential.

- For me, it is all about choice and the freedom to create whatever lifestyle, income, and quality of life you desire. It is important that you compensate your team well, give them constant training to nurture their passion, and help develop their skills.

- Always delegate their role based on their strengths. Motivate with incentives they can look forward to. Inspire them to be part of a mission that is bigger than individuals and possible only with the help of their hearts and contribution. Honor who they are, those who came before, and those who stay. They are all God's angels and blessings in your life. They are your *purpose* family.

A MESSAGE OF APPRECIATION

Receive this appreciation for the times you have served. Please know that every act of kindness is the universal bank of contribution. There is nothing you have given or shared that is not been seen by the eye of God. The Universe is counting each and every time. The stars are in alignment to see you succeed. Angels are surrounding you to protect your path. You have nothing to worry about, just keep a clean heart.

CHAPTER 11

Abundance: The Fountain of Infinite Joy

Most people have a past—a story to tell about painful moments and events they have experienced and severe circumstances they (hopefully) have overcome. Previously in this book, I shared my story with you about surviving and overcoming violence. You are aware that I am a mother of twin boys, one of whose life was threatened by a lethal disease at only eight days old and by being born prematurely.

My family has had a history of pain and suffering for generations. Even after all of this, I came to realize that my past experiences were a part of cultivating a life of happiness and abundance. In this last chapter, I will tell you how you have access to the source that will enable you to create your best life right now. Once you discover the beauty and blessing in your most painful experiences, your life and your blessings will shift and expand.

It's time to see what happened to you as part of a lesson, a plan for you to help others through your *purpose* and see your past as a treasure. This is what a life of transformation is all about! My life's *purpose* gave a new meaning to my past. Once I discovered my *purpose*, I discovered I had significant growth and development, and my outlook on my past was modified to view it now as the perfection of my pain through the love of God. Because of this, I can teach and coach any person no matter what difficult situation they have gone through.

Living your mission leads you to realize that your capacity for success and your light were always there, even in the darkest hours of your life. As you discover and share your gifts, you'll discover the abundance of opportunity, peace, and financial success within you.

You may ask, "How do you manifest of a life of abundance for yourself?" It does not matter your current status. Whether you are struggling financially or living and experiencing the best time of your life, it is a perfect time for you to receive the prosperity you truly deserve. Regardless of whether you are going through a dark tunnel or you are in a blissful state of light, use the following distinctions to unleash your power to claim what is already yours.

THE VEIL

To create abundance, we must first understand what was blocking it. Contrary to what many coaches teach, I don't think your relationships with prosperity, money, resources, and happiness are a matter of your mindset. Beliefs are superficial, so when you change them, you create an impact. Unless you know the root of the cause of your issues, this will only be a temporary fix. By identifying, working with, and addressing any outstanding emotional roots, you will see the manifestation of the abundance you know you deserve. If it's no longer a belief and you know it is not a root, what is it? It is a *veil.*

A veil is an invisible vibration that the Ego will use against you. The veil is so transparent that it cannot be seen by you. It is like the background music in an important movie scene—you can feel the impact, but you are not focused on it because you are focused on what is happening in the movie. The main mission of the veil is to block your prosperity.

When you are living your *purpose*, your Ego will use other strategies to interfere with your prosperity. It will become even harder to identify its activities unless you know how it evolves. It is always evolving as much as you do.

Examples of Veils:

- You have given your word to an important commitment. You know the time and date. When it gets closer, you start thinking you don't want to do it. You start hearing the reasons in your mind to ignore your commitment. When you overcome your thoughts using some necessary self-coaching, the Ego will proceed to activate the veil. You will no longer hear the voices in your head; however, you will start feeling like you do not want to complete your assigned tasks. This is when your Ego gets tricky. Many who are in tune with their feelings will think it is a sign to change your decision, but it is the opposite. If your Essence has already said *yes* to something, honor it even if you don't feel like it. By honoring your word, you will find the confirmation of why you made this choice. When you don't honor your word, your abundance is in jeopardy.

- When you are good at making money, producing sales, and attracting business, it is easier for the financial veil to appear in forms of affirmations like, "I am good at making money, but not managing money." This rationale and reasoning are justified by the veil. This is similar to you accepting that you have permission to be irresponsible and are not a good steward of your money because you are already good at making it. This is a large obstacle you will have to surpass as you move forward and obtain abundance by living your *purpose*.

- When you really care about helping people and serving them, the veil of "money is not important" takes shape as a way to keep you from receiving the compensation you deserve.

- The veil of not speaking up for yourself will take form when you are a person who likes to keep peace and harmony between people. People with this veil don't get paid what they deserve, and they don't stand against injustice being done to them. They let others take advantage of them.

ESSENCE REMINDER

Recognizing the veil is the first and most important step. The second step is to stop, breathe, and listen to your Essence. Now, lift your veil!

Homeplay:

Reflect on what abundance veils you can find in your life. Write down at least two of them and what types of actions you will take to lift each veil.

ABUNDANCE ROADMAP

1. I invite you to see the abundance that already exists in your life. When you are grateful for the gifts already present, you are telling the Universe you are ready for more.

2. There are different types of abundance:

    - **Your health:** Health is one of your biggest assets. Without it, you cannot enjoy any material abundance.

    - **Your family:** Everything you receive would be meaningless without the love of your family.

    - **Your God-given friends:** A true friend is a true treasure.

    - **Your *purpose:*** You already know that without *purpose*, nothing matters. Your *purpose* is your biggest source of abundance.

- **Your connection with God, Essence:** Your peace has no price.
- **Your Essence:** Material abundance. These are gifts and resources that are given to you.
- **Your money:** The ultimate compensation for sharing your *purpose* with the world.

3. Every experience in your life comes with a lesson. The lesson comes with compensation as well. That is abundance.
4. Your past experiences are an asset for your future.
5. People are willing to pay to learn from your wisdom. Don't be afraid to ask for what you deserve.
6. Your darkest moments were training you to serve and inspire others. The chapters of the book of your life are a part of the wisdom you have experienced. Many others may read it and learn from you and your book of knowledge.
7. Create a transformational business empire with your *purpose*. Every calling has a manifestation in a service or product for others.
8. Welcome your challenges with gratitude, knowing that a gift is coming your way, so you may serve others in a better, bigger way.

9. A challenge is a sign that God has a blessing in store for you to unlock.

10. Review your life and do a transformational check daily. This is to supervise which areas of your life are led by your Essence/heart and which areas are led by your Ego. How do you know? Just check your results.

11. Don't fear the darkness of the unknown or challenging situations! Your infinite light will always be brighter than any dark tunnel. No matter what obstacles or challenges you may face, there is always an open exit waiting for you. Let your light shine so you can find your way towards your *purpose* and your success.

12. Be alert for the revelation of hidden secrets. There are many more things that are part of the universal treasure of the world. You must claim your share!

BUILDING AN EMPIRE

The plane was taxiing down the runway and I was on my way to the bright lights of sunny California. I was pondering the next step for my life *purpose* while reading a powerful business book called *Zero to One* by Peter Thiel. During my reverie, I was looking for signs of acknowledgement of what should be my next move.

I discovered that when we are living our *purpose,* God is always giving us messages to let us know what's there for us. I started having a sensation in my heart when I got to the part where Peter was talking about the invisible secrets that are not yet revealed.

God will make visible the multibillion-dollar businesses that have yet to be created and are invisible to the majority of people. We will be able to identify and know our multibillion-dollar ideas. While we all have access to these ideas, only a small portion of the population will understand and know how to use it. Only those who are willing to connect and stay present will have access to receiving them. This is the actual path of abundance, only available for a few who are willing to take the road to actually claim that billion-dollar idea.

That night, during a flight to California and while people slept, a multibillion-dollar idea was revealed to me. I discovered that my fifteen-year journey was preparing me for what was about to happen next. After the release of this book, you will soon know what comprised this major manifestation and my transformative idea.

Sometimes you have given a lot of time and energy and invested money in one source and you don't see the fruits in that source. But in the invisible world, you are already largely compensated, so keep doing what you know is right. Be in integrity. Clean up your space. As soon as you claim it, you will see the Universe transfer abundance to you. The transfer will be in the form of your multibillion-dollar idea.

So how do you receive this transfer? You reflect on what the need is in the world right now that people don't know they have, but if you were to solve it, it will already be solved when they need it. For example, we didn't know we needed mobile phones, cars, or airplanes until they were created. We didn't know how much we needed the internet, or to read and write, until they were created. These things were revealed to those who were ready.

Now use your hands to either work hard for your abundance or allow the Universe to give you your share. The moment you marry your *purpose* and start living it, you become a shareholder in the universal funds. It is up to you if you want to claim the funds—they are there. When you become part of the 1 percent who are living their *purpose*, you have access to the funds available to those who are living their *purpose*. This multibillion-dollar *purpose* will be given to you.

I confirmed this, because I soon as I received my idea, I met with my coaching client and friend, Liz Stern, and I shared my idea with her. Within fifteen minutes, she agreed to be an investor of the company. Those fifteen minutes were life-changing. They represented the two *years* of our relationship. As soon as we presented our idea as partners to our prospective investor, he decided to invest millions of dollars in our company. In less than a month, I went from having a great idea, to having a vision that became the reality of a multimillion-dollar business. The fruit of what I had been working on for the past fifteen years was manifested in only thirty days. What a blessing!

The developing of your *purpose* into measurable abundance is like what happens with a Chinese bamboo tree. Like the tree, your *purpose* requires nurturing. Your *purpose* needs to be planted in fertile soil and receive the food necessary to make it grow tall and strong. For five to seven years, the Chinese bamboo tree does not show any signs of germinating. There is nothing happening on the surface. Yet, when it does happen, there is exponential and miraculous growth of between eighty and ninety feet in a just few weeks.

You may ask how a tree could grow to be that tall in such a brief period of time. There was a foundation and groundwork being cultivated underneath the soil, behind the scenes, providing all that was necessary to ensure abundant growth. This is you, you are the tree. Everything you have lived, shared, learned, experienced, trained for, cried over, suffered, everything that put you down, brought you back up, every place you traveled to, everything you observed, connected to, envisioned, dreamed of, talked about, studied, reflected on, meditated over, or are grateful for will come to form your roots, the roots of your *purpose.*

ESSENCE REMINDER

Every person who is willing to persevere and do what is necessary to fulfill his *purpose* is destined to be successful. There is no other way.

CONSPIRACY ANGELS

Once you are living your life *purpose*, you start encountering a series of conspiracy experiences in your favor. People will consider you *lucky,* yet this has nothing to do with luck. Leaders that are fulfilling their mission and sharing their gifts with the world love helping others.

You will meet and attract other people who will be on the same quest because they will share the same vibration as you. They will believe in you and are willing to share their secrets and tools with you so you can learn too. They will give you a hand and sometimes even invest money in your vision, business, and needs. I call this group *conspiracy angels*. They come from different backgrounds, and sometimes you will meet them in the least expected places. This is the universal team given to you as a token of appreciation for ranking higher, moving forward, and being part of the 1 percent of leaders living their life's *purpose*.

When Connecting with Your Conspiracy Angels

- Keep your eyes open, and most importantly, your heart.
- Make sure you will always include the topic of your *purpose* in every conversation. Every person you meet may be a conspiracy angel or may lead you to one.
- You must be clear of your *purpose*, your vision, mission.
- Provide *clarity* of your plan of action over the next five years.
- Provide *clarity* of what you need, what type of resources you are seeking.
- When having conversations about *purpose,* detect others' *purpose* too. Confirm where they are in the process and that they are living it. Ask yourself what resources or contribution you may bring to them.

COLLECTIVE EGO CONSPIRACY

The same way you will identify conspiracy angels on your *purpose* quest, you will find a collective Ego conspiring to obstruct your legacy of abundance. These collective Egos may be in the form of jealous, envious people, others may be offended by your presence, some critics may be trying to discredit your work, and so on.

The collective Ego conspiracy can also show up in the form of last-minute interruptions when significant and important positions are about to happen for you. A deeper work of this conspiracy is when the Ego interferes through family members or friends you really love. The Ego conspiracy is trying to convince your family and friends to persuade you to forgo and not trust your process or the people you are working with, even when you know in your heart you are on the right path.

Many times, the Ego will wait patiently for you to make a mistake in order to jump right in and begin building a case of negativity that will pit others against you. When leaders are not prepared, they can be discouraged by this form of the Ego which creates an obstacle to the manifestation of their abundance.

When Facing the Collective Ego Conspiracy

- Don't be surprised—the Ego loves to get you off center, off guard. Acknowledge that the situation is just part of your new position of power. Every powerful leader has his/her amount of Ego conspiracy. If you don't have one, you are not doing something impactful enough!

- Act in spite of fear. You may be feeling weak sometimes, a feeling of discomfort in your stomach. Breathe in and out three times. Say to your Ego's little voice in your heart "Thank you for sharing, thank you for reminding me that I am strong. I am the chosen one and my *purpose* is meant to be, no matter what!"
- If you have made a mistake, clean it up, taking responsibility, and restore your integrity. Great leaders know you are not perfect and if you apologize and admit your faults, others know they can trust you.
- Speak up when you hear or find out something that is not true about you or other people. Do not let your Ego get away with what it wants. Cleaning up also means taking a stand for what is right.
- Be patient. Great things take divine time, which means perfect timing. Trust the process and the intervention of the visible and invisible conspiracy angels. They are working even harder when the collective Ego is present.

HARVARD UNIVERSITY—A STORY OF CONSPIRACY

Years ago, I received a call from a well-known Harvard Club director confirming that I was booked to speak at Harvard University for the Wealth and Happiness Summit. I was so excited and grateful! Harvard University, for me, meant a whole new level of edification for my Essence, my work, and my *purpose*. Ready to deliver a powerful message, I was going to give it my all as tears of joy coursed down my face.

We spent the next four weeks coordinating the logistics of the event through myriad conference calls with the production team and directors. Everything was ready for this speaking engagement. I made the public announcements in social media, press releases were sent out announcing I would be speaking at Harvard on November 2nd. I thought everything was going fantastically well. Two weeks before my presentation, I received a call that my keynote speech was postponed until next year, and that they were going to "get back to me" with the time when this was going to happen.

I was numb and in shock. I didn't really receive an explanation; I knew something was up. I racked my brain and just couldn't figure out what it was. In my mind I was confused and somewhat disappointed, yet in my heart God's voice was saying, "Karen, everything will be okay."

"Yes, I know everything is going to be okay, but this does not give me back the keynote at Harvard," my Ego replied. I chose to trust and let the conspiracy angels do their work. Fast-forward four months later. I was a guest keynote speaker for my friend Bill Walsh at one of his business expos. A man approached me from the audience. This participant was from Harvard; I did not recognize him because all our communications had been over the phone. He recognized me, however. After the presentation was over and many rushed to hug and thank me, this participant made it through the masses of people huddled around me to let me know who he was. He said, "Karen, you are coming to Harvard, this time is a must, they need to hear your powerful message, let's talk." I thanked him. This was what I was manifesting.

After a short follow-up, only a month later I was speaking at Harvard University, this time at an even higher level than was planned before. The audience was Harvard University professors and I was the only speaker at this event. You can see the entire keynote online. The professors went from being closed-arms and formal to being totally open with tears in their eyes by the end of my seminar. Harvard loved my training so much they invited me back again within sixty days.

You may be asking, "What happened before?" I got the answer after becoming good friends with the leader from Harvard. He shared with me that after having everything ready for my presentation in November, a well-known speaker called him directly to tell him not to have me speak because I was a diva, too much to deal with, and thought I belonged on a red carpet not on the prestigious Harvard stage. (I won't mention who this person is so as not to give extra publicity to someone who can do such a thing.)

My now-friend told me he felt trapped, and because he didn't want to say no to such a high-caliber coach and speaker, he decided to cancel my presentation. My friend even confessed that he hadn't been planning to invite me ever again. But after listening and watching me in action, he knew in his heart that no matter what some people may think, I was the perfect match for what he was looking for and even much better than he thought.

From my keynotes at Harvard, I received many new clients, opportunities, and edification of my brand that led to much more financial abundance and a big lesson of faith and how protected we are when doing what is right and walking with God in our hearts with our conspiracy angels.

We will be covered all the way. Nothing will be taken away; the abundance will be multiplying when we stand by our *purpose*. Even if the circumstances look really bad, the collective Ego of darkness will be always outnumbered by the Essence light of God!

REFERENCES OF A MIRACLE

> *My life was turned completely upside down. My family and I were totally wiped out physically and only had the clothes on our backs, and I was literally down to my last five dollars as a direct result of Hurricane Sandy. Then the most unexpected miracle happened, someone provided me with gift that would change my life—the opportunity to participate in Karen's seminar. Within two weeks of my graduation, over twenty thousand dollars that I had been waiting on for months suddenly came to me. I left my job at an unfulfilling business and went full-time into living my purpose. After I took these initial steps, I was able to manifest over forty thousand dollars' worth of home repairs and obtained a new car. The total financial blessings to my family within three months of the seminar have exceeded one hundred thousand dollars.*
>
> —*Mark Dana, Entrepreneur*

As you can see in Mark's case, *purpose* abundance can be radical once you clean your space. Money is energy and it will follow your own energy. If your energy is in your mind, money will become an illusion that you will often miss. If your energy is in your Essence, the manifestation of money will be tangible and accessible to you. Sometimes even a natural disaster that appears to be against you is a conspiracy in your favor. Every challenging time is a gift in disguise.

Abundance in all forms circulates through your space all day long. Take the time to feel the experience of having it all, for you already do. When greeting people, declare that they are amazing, that you and they are blessed. May your attitude towards life reflect the vibration of your faith. Conspiracy angels love high-level energy and passionate leaders.

THE FOUNTAIN OF INFINITE JOY

What I have shared with you in this book is the ultimate path to your *purpose*. Infinite joy is a constant feeling of peace and the knowledge that no matter what, you will be okay if you choose to be faithful to your *purpose*. This feeling is in the background of everything that is happening in your life.

You will have the perfect peace and knowledge that even if everything falls apart, you know God is with you no matter what.

When you are living your *purpose*, what is meant to be for you, no one can take away from you. It may change forms, it may not come to you from the people or the resource from which you thought it would come, but you still will receive it because it is already named for you. What belongs to you, no one can take.

HONOR IT

Even if everything you have disappears from in front of your eyes, it does not disappear from the multiple realms of possibilities of the Universe of your *purpose*, and it is there waiting to be claimed once again by you. Once something comes back to you, it comes in an even better form.

It is easy to feel joy and excitement when everything is happening and the world is positive. What I want to bring to you is the ability to access joy in spite of any challenging situation.

When I was starting to follow my dreams to become a coach and speaker, I had my last savings of about twelve thousand dollars. I was getting divorced, and my children were less than a year old. I met an owner of a taxicab service in New York. Coming from Colombia, it is known as a good source of residual income to have a taxi business. Drivers will drive the taxis for you, the driver gets paid, and you will also—a win-win situation. This was what this taxicab service owner promised me. Because I decided to follow my passion and fulfill my *purpose*, I was seeking a way to support my family while building my vision. This man said he would give me one thousand dollars a month in residual income. I believed him. I received a handwritten receipt and I moved on, focused on my mission. Several weeks passed and I didn't hear from him. After many months, I never saw him again.

My Ego and mind were screaming "You will never live your *purpose*, you are so stupid, you're done." In spite of all the negative thoughts, I was feeling something different. I found myself in a deep peace with a new sense of tranquility despite this terrible situation. It didn't make sense to me.

I had this peace and a knowingness that everything was going to be okay. Even though the results were showing something different, there was there a new sense of tranquility that I didn't have before living my *purpose.* I knew right then that no matter how difficult a situation would be, I was going to go through it and overcome any obstacle. Why? Because I heard God's voice speak to me clearly in my heart, saying "Karen, everything will be okay. You're not alone, I am with you."

I thought I would be heartbroken, devastated, and depressed. Instead, all felt was God's love.

I discovered that God was with me, not only as a form of a belief but as a living fact. I began to truly feel God's presence even in the most challenging part of the beginning of my mission. I hadn't had this type of access prior to living my *purpose.* I knew I was home.

Since living my calling, I now listen to God and hear him at any time. Overcoming our challenges is the process of evolution. When we grow, we evolve. The challenges may temporarily knock you down, but like a phoenix rising from the ashes of the combustion, you will find that you will be delivered from your desperation. You will experience and receive unconditional love. God will uncover masterly and impressive Essence conspiracy angels that will come to you when you need them the most.

God is so much on your side that when you feel you can't go on, God will give you a sign. He will provide water when you are thirsty, food when you are hungry, and strength when you are weak. You must simply trust. You will no longer feel alone. This experience will provide you with the opportunity to know your true self. The fountain of infinite joy is your connection with God and the profound peace that this provides to the manifestation of your *purpose*.

IN CASE OF EMERGENCY

When facing the inevitable dark moments that you will encounter living your *purpose*, make sure you know that these are shaping you into your greater self. It is not that God is against you, it is the opposite.

ESSENCE REMINDER

God lets us go through challenges so we can grow into the best version of who we are.

What can you do when everything seems to be flowing and something difficult happens unexpectedly? To expect the unexpected and be comfortable with it is part of our process of consciousness. As we move into acceptance versus resistance of the unknown challenges in store for us, we also develop an extraordinary ability to manifest solutions immediately. This allows us to unlock the infinite gifts in store for us in the Universal Bank.

When facing any challenging time, take the following steps moving forward:

- Breathe. When in shock, the body usually wants to shut down to avoid pain. Feel the feelings that you are experiencing and be aware of your emotions (even if it's deep sadness). Don't reject your emotions. Embrace them and transmute them into energy for your growth. Do this while breathing consciously. Your body will automatically relax and feel better.

- o Now you can think better.

- Ask for help! There are multiple skillful and outstanding angels waiting to support you in this process. Call someone. Don't keep your emotions to yourself, this is exactly what your Ego wants. Let it all out and share them. Inform the person how you really feel and express yourself knowing that it is going to help you help feel better.
- Stay still and listen to God's voice within you. Now that you have let your Ego express itself, it's time for you to really listen to what your Essence has to say.
- Your Essence is always talking to you. God is always talking to you.
- When you are living your life *purpose*, you open a direct line of communication with God that allows you to clearly hear what He has to say.
- You will become like the eye of the storm. In the center, it is still and quiet and on the outside it's chaos.
- You can't stop chaos from happening, but what you can do is to choose God when facing chaos.

- God knows exactly what you need.
- Go beyond the mind that is telling you to give up.
- The Ego always wants to try to find reasons to give up. Don't give power to those reasons.
- Surrender to God's voice and hear Him when he says, "I'm here with you. You're not alone, and you will never be."

Homeplay

Abundance Meter

To manifest a constant flow of abundance in all areas of life, we must check our meters to make sure our abundance vibration is in place. There are many ways to measure this vibration and many actions we can take to adjust it if necessary.

Ask yourself the following questions and answer them with Essence and authenticity:

1. Do you truly *believe* you deserve abundance in your life?

    - If the answer is *yes*, write down three results in your life that support your *yes* and three actions you will take to ensure this abundance will continue growing throughout your life's *purpose.*
    - If the answer is *no*, follow the steps of self-coaching in chapter six to find the root of your unhealthy relationship with prosperity.

2. Do you *feel* that you already live in abundance?

    - If the answer is *yes*, write down in detail three different times you felt abundance in the past week.

    - If the answer is *no*, follow the steps of self-coaching in chapter six to find the root of your unhealthy relationship with abundance.

3. What habits do you have right now that are not congruent with the universal abundance you deserve? Write down the top three and the actions you will take to transform them.

4. Create a list of events, people, and experiences you will accomplish in the next week that will contribute to the manifestation of your Essence abundance.

PRACTICAL SPIRITUALITY

As you move forward to a new life of *purpose*, your consciousness expands, and the awareness of your actions becomes sharper. You can easily see yourself and recognize when you are not being your authentic self, even when you are going back and forth from Ego to Essence.

Now that you are in a higher level of presence with your conscience and your Essence, you are experiencing the evolution of the effects of your unconscious. The Universe is on your side, the conspiracy angels are there to serve you and to face the darkness. You are protected to fulfill your *purpose*.

HONOR IT

If you decide to listen to your mind and take actions that are not congruent, this will no longer have just the regular energetic boomerang effect in the particular area of the action, it will directly impact your abundance, especially your health and finances. You were born to live a healthy, happy, joyful, and prosperous life. This is your destiny and only you have the power to change that. To ensure that you will contribute to the edification of your blissful life, take these steps:

- Take a close look at any unresolved situations. These can be conversations you haven't had yet. Even if they are minor, if you are thinking about it, it is in your space and it is draining your abundance vibration.

- Take full responsibility for any financial commitments you may still have pending, even if they are small in your eyes. Talk to people, negotiate, and create payment plans, even if small to start with. If you move this energy, the abundance will start coming your way even faster so you can honor everything and continue serving your *purpose*. You must be willing to be impeccable.

- The Universal Prosperity Diamond Rule is no longer optional here. Remember regarding your income: donate 10 percent, save 10 percent to invest, and have a 100 percent clarity system to know what is coming in and going out.

- Donate your time. Every month, find ways to plant abundance seeds by donating your time and wisdom to those who need it and may never get access to your gift. This does not mean you don't value your time, and in fact it is the opposite, because it is a treasure you also choose to invest it in humanity through your legacy.

- Do unexpected acts of kindness. Clean someone's car, pay someone's bills, tip the entire amount of your check, celebrate your birthday with kids in hospitals, pick up garbage in the streets, let someone go first in line, and so on. Be creative. Remember the words of Mother Teresa, "It is not the magnitude of our actions but the amount of love that is put into them that matters."

- Share your knowledge with those who need it. Don't take any secrets with you. Create both nonprofit and for-profit ways to share your wisdom.

- Start and finish your day with gratitude for your abundance. Create an intention every day for the manifestation of your *purpose.*

- In your daily prayer, meditate to bring the energy and visualization of abundance into every area of your life.

TRANSFORMATIONAL ABUNDANCE PRAYER

God, as I walk through the ultimate quest, I recognize the perfection of every step that leads me here and now. As I swim in the deep waters of my own transformation, I hear Your voice everywhere I go. I experience the awakening of my Essence. I feel the pain and joy of humanity within. I find compassion and the inspiration to take unstoppable actions.

God, bless me with the strength I need to face the collective Ego and every obstacle that appears big to the illusions of my mind.

I follow Your guidance as I have surrendered to Your *purpose* in my life. I am in love with my mission, with my experiences, and with the gifts You have given me to honor Your legacy. I no longer doubt, even if my mind does. I am no longer afraid, even if my mind is inundated by the fears of my past. I am no longer a slave to my Ego, for I have found You in my heart.

I am present to Your love and abundance all around. I can hear the music of nature and receive its power, accessible to me in generous forms. I embrace my whole being and every part of it, the light and the darkness, for this makes me whole. I kiss the present, I love my body and nurture it like the temple it is. The movement of my soul is reflected in the movements of my head, arms, and feet. I open my arms to receive all Your gifts, for I am no longer in the way of your manifestation.

God, give me the courage to stand for Your vision, to ignite the passion within me to share my voice no matter what. God, bless my family, friends, and every person on Earth with the abundance we all deserve. I am present of my influence and the full impact of my actions. God, give me the discerning clarity to choose my Essence with every important question I face.

I am blessed. I am abundance, I live in abundance, and I bring abundance to the world. Universe of power, I accept your magic and use it for good. God, surround me with angels, warriors of light, action allies of *purpose*. I breathe the oxygen of multiple possibilities given at every second to choose what is best for me and the world. I am a master of masters and my wisdom is only given to me through the channeling of Your word. I am a force of peace and unity. I am the one.

om shanti, om

ESSENCE REMINDER

Om is the sound of the Universe. *Shanti* is a Sanskrit word that means "peace."

"Om shanti, shanti, shanti." The latter symbolizes three forms of peace: peace of the mind, peace in speech, and peace in the physical body.

You have now opened the gates of the infinite source of abundance. I trust that you will use this power to share it with those who need it the most. We are walking together as we recognize that our *purpose* only happens in oneness. I am your *purpose* and you are mine. When the illusion of separation disappears, the Essence of who we really are arises. Only love is present.

As we reach this beautiful space, we know this is not the ending, it is a new beginning. I thank you from my heart for allowing me to touch and open your heart and share my *purpose* with you. I send you my love and energy, trusting that God will guide every step you take. Re-read this book from time to time.

HONOR IT

You will find many new principles, for you are always evolving. I am here for you. I am your coach to serve you in the manifestation of your *purpose* today and for the rest of my life.

I love you and I believe in you,
Namaste,
Karen Hoyos

P.S. I have a very special gift for you. To receive it, please visit my website: www.KarenHoyos.com

ABOUT THE AUTHOR

Karen Hoyos is a global transformational leader, celebrity coach, speaker, and successful entrepreneur who has reached millions of people through her seminars, top television show appearances, published articles, and best-selling products. She personally coaches Hollywood celebrities, athletes, politicians, and entrepreneurs.